Understanding Archaeological Excavation

Understanding Archaeological Excavation

Philip Barker

St. Martin's Press   NEW YORK

All rights reserved. For information, write:
Scholary & Reference Division,
St. Martin's Press, Inc., 175 Fifth Avenue, New York, NY 10010

First published in the United States of America in 1986

Printed in Great Britain

ISBN 0–312–83078–5

Library of Congress Cataloguing-in-Publication Data

Barker, Philip (Philip A.)
Understanding archaeological excavation.

Bibliography: p.
Includes index.
1. Archaeology—Field work.   2. Excavations
(Archaeology)   I. Title
CC76.B373   1986   930.1   86–10117
ISBN 0–312–83078–5

CONTENTS

ACKNOWLEDGEMENTS

Thanks are due to the many colleagues and friends who have given permission for their photographs and drawings to be used, often in advance of publication. In particular, Philip Rahtz, Arnold Baker, Dominic Powlesland and Sidney Renow were most generous in supplying illustrations. I am also grateful to John Schofield, Chris Musson, Bill and Jenny Britnell, Jan Wills, Brian Hobley, Francis Pryor, Susan Laflin Barker, W.A. van Es, Charles Hill, Axel Steensberg, Hans-Emil Liden, Peter Boland, Steven Linnane, Wayne Cocroft, Robert Higham, Shaun Goddard, John Allen, Martin Carver, Clive Partridge, John Williams, Rupert Bruce-Mitford, Peter Scholefield, Freddie Charles, Martin Charles, James Dinn, and Marion and Kevin Blockley. Heather Bird made original drawings for figures 2-6, 9 and 10, and Jacqui Barker typed with all her fingers what I had typed with three.

This book would have been much poorer, if not impossible, without their help.

PREFACE

This book is written for everyone who has ever looked over the fence at an archaeological excavation and wondered how the diggers could make a coherent story out of the mud and rubble, the fragments of wall, the layers of clay or acres of gravel riddled with pits and criss-crossed by ditches.

The best way to understand an excavation is to join one, to trowel and to barrow, to help wash pottery and bones, to hold the surveying staff and to plot the outlines of features and the intricacies of surfaces. But some cannot take an active part and some want an insight into the complications of the art before they join an excavation. This book is for them also.

The amount of archaeological literature published these days is immense, beyond the capacity of any one person to read in a lifetime, ranging from wild speculations on the meaning of Stonehenge to highly specialised monographs on single aspects of complex sites. Accordingly, the list of recommended books has been kept as short as possible. Most of them, however, contain their own bibliographies, so that the reader can pursue a line of thought or enquiry into the far depths of the subject.

In some respects, this book is an expansion of Chapter 3, 'Excavation' in Kevin Greene's book in the same series, *Archaeology, An Introduction*, and should be read in conjunction with his book, which describes, in greater detail than here, the development of archaeology, non-destructive site examination, dating methods and the scientific analysis of excavated material.

Why do we dig?
We do not often stop to consider that we are the only species of animal that realizes it has a past, that can consciously consider it and has a compelling urge to find out more about it.

We are intensely curious about everything around us and have probably been so since the very earliest times. This curiosity has led to the study of the natural world, from the structure of the atom to the exploration of deep space, and from the living cell to the vagaries of human behaviour. This same curiosity has led men to wonder and speculate about the past, and particularly, from the point of view of this book, about the visible remains of earlier societies which were everywhere around them. The most primitive peoples invent rich and wonderful legends to explain the creation of the world and the development of their society. These legends bear only a mythological relationship to the long and slow evolution which each of these societies has gone through and it is only recently, perhaps as recently as the Renaissance, that men have tried to piece together a logical and coherent history from the physical remains of the past, as distinct from oral tradition and written histories.

As individuals we may at first be interested only in our own immediate past – our parents and grandparents, great-aunts and uncles, the places our families have lived in, their occupations, their origins. Those of us who assume that our ancestors have lived for many generations in the same country may be happy to immerse ourselves in our country's history, as being our own. Others, immigrants or emigrants, may want more specific detail, as, for instance, the thousands of Americans who search for their ancestors in Europe, or, a more spectacular example, Arthur Haley describing in *Roots* how he traced his forebears back to their ancestral tribe in Africa.

But man's interest in the past transcends the history of individuals. For some there is an addiction to historical novels or the recreation of past battles; others visit museums or tour ancient sites in Europe and beyond, while millions watch 'historical' television programmes from *Chronicle* and *Timewatch* to wildly anachronistic films, as when Kirk Douglas, a Viking with an axe in each hand, attacks a late medieval castle. There is an almost insatiable appetite for the past in all its aspects.

One of the tasks of the historian and the archaeologist is to modify our view of the past by continual reconsideration of the evidence and, in the case of the archaeologist particularly, the production of new evidence. For the many thousands of years before the invention of writing and the first surviving documents, whether in stone or clay or papyrus, archaeological evidence is all we have. Increasingly in later centuries, documentary evidence must be married to the archaeological evidence, which is continually expanding in scope and complexity. By contrast, it is unlikely that there are many ancient manuscripts left to be discovered. Inscriptions will be dug up from time to time; some more Dead Sea scrolls may be found, and, like the Haydn Mass recently discovered in Ireland, a precious manuscript may be waiting to be revealed, but there is little doubt that, in the future, new information about the past will derive chiefly from archaeology, and from field work and excavation in particular. The purpose of excavation is therefore to solve, or at least to throw light on, problems which can be studied in no other way, since there is an absolute limit to the amount one can learn from an archaeological site by looking at it, walking over it, surveying it or photographing it from the air, just as there is a limit to the inferences which can be drawn from documentary references (where they exist) to archaeological sites. Only excavation can uncover a sequence of structures or recover stratified and secure dating evidence, or the mass of environmental or economic evidence which most sites contain.

The multiplicity of disciplines which go to make up modern archaeology combine to study every aspect of the lives of early peoples – their environment, their trade, their diet, the rise and fall of individual settlements and groups of settlements, their cultural affinities, the influences which shaped their buildings and their art – to look beyond the objects and the debris of everyday life to the thoughts that lay behind them, and the intentions that produced them.

The chief function of the excavator is, therefore, to produce primary evidence of as high a quality as possible for the use of other archaeologists, historians, and all those whose interest lies in understanding the past.

The very opacity of the soil – the fact that we do not know what it hides until we dig it – is perhaps the most compelling reason for becoming an excavator. It is forensic science without the criminal, detective work which tries to establish something of the truth about the people of the past from the ruins of their buildings and their rubbish, and sometimes from their own remains. It requires a detached attitude of stringent logic allied to a vigorous imagination which can conjure, without fantasy, buildings from lines of stones and people from the trinkets they wore and the meat bones they threw away. It often feels like putting together a jigsaw puzzle with only a tenth of the pieces and without a picture on the lid of the box; but if we had the lid of the box we wouldn't bother to do the jigsaw, and we are happy to go on discovering and fitting together the pieces without any real expectation of finishing the picture, but always of improving it.

CHAPTER ONE

How archaeological sites are formed

It is much easier to understand the evidence recovered from excavations if we appreciate the ways in which archaeological sites are formed: how a castle becomes an earthwork, or a Roman town a field of corn; how a prehistoric village becomes a series of dark green lines seen only in the spring – though not every year; and how a modern city's past can be buried under tons of concrete yet still be recovered.

The surface of the earth is almost entirely covered by soil which derives from the underlying bedrock, be it sand, gravel, chalk, granite, clay or any other rock, hard or soft. The nature of the soil cover is determined, therefore, by the rock on which it lies, and this, combined with the drainage of the subsoil, will in turn determine the fertility of the soil, which, in its turn, will influence the patterns of vegetation, of farming and of settlement.

Weathering, erosion, decay, collapse and the invasion of every kind of plant and animal life continually combine to reduce all man-made structures once more to soil so that it is with soil that the excavator chiefly has to deal. The archaeologist has to be as familiar with soils as a farmer, to be sensitive to changes of colour and texture in layers that look superficially the same; to attempt to understand the derivation of each layer that he encounters; to recognize, for instance, the difference between naturally deposited layers on the one hand, and earth dumped to build up the ground level on the other; and to be aware of the effects that different soils have on the objects buried in them. For example, soil with high acidity (i.e. with a low pH) will often destroy all the animal bones on the site. Unless he realizes this, the excavator might mistakenly assume that there were no domestic animals or animals used for food there. Under these circumstances, human burials are often reduced to mere stains and their presence only known from the grave itself and perhaps a badly eroded brooch or knife. Excavators have been misled by formations of 'iron-pan' (see glossary) into believing them to be floors, even iron-working floors, though their formation is purely natural.

It will be seen, therefore, that excavators need to be soil scientists, even if only in an elementary way. The standard work on archaeological soil science is by Susan Limbrey (Limbrey, 1975) and those who are interested in pursuing this aspect further are recommended to read it.

Visitors to archaeological sites will often hear excavators talk about the 'natural', and most archaeological excavations stop when they reach the 'natural'. This is excavator's jargon for the undisturbed subsoil. It is, in many ways, a misleading term, since it is possible, for instance, for occupation layers to be covered by silts brought down by a river, or washed down from a hill above the site. Such silts are certainly 'natural' but they must, of course, be treated as part of the site's history and removed to reveal the underlying occupation. Establishing the unequivocal presence of the subsoil is often difficult and may require excavation into the subsoil in order to examine it well below possible occupation levels. Sometimes the subsoil is so difficult to identify that it needs the advice of a professional soil scientist. Such advice may also be needed to determine whether layers have been dumped or have silted naturally, or whether ditches or hollows have been filled by water-borne or wind-blown deposits.

As will become increasingly apparent throughout this book, modern excavations can no longer be the work of inspired individuals with gangs of labourers, but require teams of specialists, working together to a common end.

Archaeological sites are merely the residues of settlements and structures, reduced to rubble and earthworks by decay, erosion, stone-robbing and the invasions of plant and animal life. Even in temperate Britain the 'jungle' returns with astonishing speed to an abandoned garden or a neglected copse. Bombed sites in city centres were colonized within a few months, and there are places known to the writer where almost impenetrable woodland cloaks ruined cottages inhabited only half a century ago.

Stone buildings, even deeply robbed ones, leave more evidence of their presence than wooden ones, which may be reduced to no more than a line of dark pits, or a barely discernible discoloration of the soil, or concentration of stones.

In order to interpret the evidence which we uncover, we need to understand as fully as possible what happens to a building when it is abandoned or is pulled down, and what happens to rubbish when it is thrown into a pit or spread as manure on the fields. We need to know how ditches and pits silt up and how banks and mounds erode, as well as something of the action of the soil on organic materials, from leather and cloth to human bodies themselves.

It is illuminating to observe what happens to a derelict building over a period of years, or the way in which plants invade an unused path, or a disused railway. Sometimes it is possible to find a recently abandoned settlement which is on its way to becoming an archaeological site and to

Fig. 1a

Fig. 1b

Fig. 1a-e *The way archaeological sites are formed*

At Blakemoorgate, on the northern end of the ridge known as the Stiper Stones in Shropshire, lies a deserted settlement. The remains of houses and outbuildings are contained within paddocks whose layered hedges have grown into trees, and the drove roads on each side of the site are overgrown with grass and gorse.

Since the site was deserted gradually, eventually leaving only one occupied farm, which was abandoned in the 1950s, the whole process of collapse and decay can be seen, from the empty farmhouse, still with its roof, **1a**, to a mound of stones and earth, **1e**, the site of a desertion of perhaps a century ago. Such a site deserves detailed survey and the recording of the memories of people, still alive, who knew it, before it goes back into the hillside.

Fig. 1c

Fig. 1d

Fig. 1e

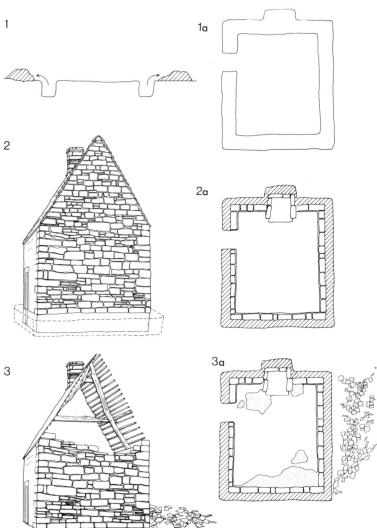

Figs. 2-4 illustrate in simplified form the construction and decay of a small stone building.

In 1 a trench is dug to take the foundations. 1a is a plan of the trench.

2 shows the completed building in the foundation trench, which has been back-filled on the outside of the wall foundations. 2a is a plan of this.

3 shows the building abandoned and losing its roof, the tiles becoming scattered at the back of the building. In 3a the floor can be seen to be beginning to break up.

In 4 the process has accelerated, and in 5, stone robbers have removed most of the stone and the usable timber and are burning the rest. The two plans 4a and 5a show the development of what will eventually become buried archaeology.

6 shows the site when the walls have become covered with soil and grass. 6a is a conjectured contour survey of this phase.

7 is a section through this phase, showing the buried walls; 8 is a section after the walls have been dug out for their stone.

9 is a section when the robber trenches have become filled up and the site is barely visible on the surface. 9a shows the plan of what would be found if the site were then excavated.

Fig. 2

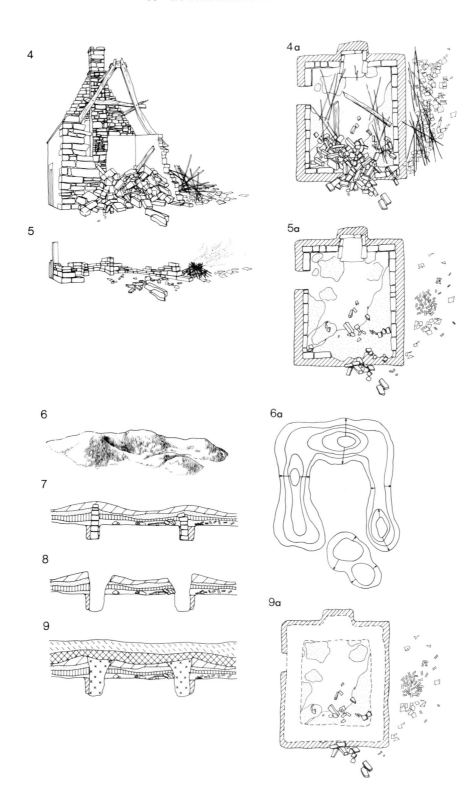

Fig. 3

Fig. 4

observe the processes of regression at work. Because of the more intensive agriculture and redevelopment of the lowlands, such sites are more often found in hill country. One such is illustrated in Fig. 1a-e. The processes of destruction and decay which transform structures into the archaeological features which we excavate can perhaps best be illustrated by simple examples which can, as it were, be multiplied up into the highly complex series of inter-related components which make up most archaeological sites. Some of the commonest features found on excavations are illustrated later in this chapter.

The other factor of major importance in the understanding of the formation of archaeological sites and their unravelling by excavation is the theory of stratification. This derives originally from the realization by geologists that those rock strata which lay uppermost were later in date than those which lay below them. In its simplest form it is easy to see that layers deposited on the bed of the sea are formed later than the rocks beneath or that a sheet of lava is later than the mountainside on which it lies. But the earth's surface is not static – rocks are thrust up through over-lying layers; erosion removes upper layers, exposing the rocks beneath; sometimes gigantic folds seem to reverse the proper order. Yet in all these cases the sequence of *events* can be understood – the intrusive rocks can be seen to be earlier, though the upheaval which caused them to become visible is later; the process of erosion is later than the rock it exposes and the folding which turns the layers upside down gives a stratification which might be misleading if it were not realized that folding had occurred.

It is the same with archaeological sites. This is most easily demonstrated by a series of superimposed floors, where it is obvious that the lower ones must be earlier. Similarly, if a roof collapses on to the uppermost floor, and then the walls fall in on top of the fallen roof, the sequence of events is again obvious and will be revealed when the layers are excavated in the reverse order to the sequence of events. The construction, abandonment and decay of a simple stone building are shown in Figs. 2-4.

These examples could be extended to cover every possible situation met with on an archaeological site. *Stratification* can be defined, therefore, as any number of relatable deposits of archaeological strata (from a stake-hole to the floor of a cathedral) which are the result of 'successive operations of either nature or mankind' (Harris 1975, 110). *Stratigraphy*, on the other hand, 'is the study of archaeological strata . . . with a view to arranging them in a chronological sequence' (Harris, *ibid*), and see pp. 142-43, Chapter 6.

HOW POST-HOLES ARE FORMED

Many timber buildings are based on posts set into the ground (rather than standing on the surface – see Figs. 82, 83). In the majority of cases, a pit is dug to the required depth and the post inserted (Fig. 5.2); the post is sometimes set against the side wall of the pit, sometimes centrally. In either case the remaining space in the pit is back-filled with the earth taken out of it, or with stones or rocks. When the building is abandoned the post can disappear in a number of different ways:

1   It can be removed. In this case it may be possible to see that it has been rocked backwards and forwards in order to loosen it to make removal easier. The hole thus left may be deliberately back-filled with earth in order, perhaps, to remove a hazard, or it may be left simply to fill up naturally. It should be possible for the excavator to tell the difference. The deliberate filling is likely to be coarser and contain stones, rather than fine silty material which has been carried by rain or wind or worm action. However, as with all the examples given here, each case will depend on factors which must be assessed on site. For example, post-holes cut in sand will have a filling which is likely itself to be sandy, whether it is deliberately or naturally filled, and in addition, very difficult to distinguish – as the excavator of the Anglo-Saxon halls at Yeavering said: 'The general distinction (between the post-hole and its filling) may best be made by calling the colour of the subsoil a very pale greyish-yellow, and that of the fillings a pale yellowish-grey.' (Hope-Taylor, 1977, 29).

2   It may be sawn off at ground level or simply left to rot. It is difficult to distinguish between these two, since in both cases the stump will be left in the ground. This will gradually be invaded by insects, moulds and bacteria, and will eventually be replaced by humic soil. This will normally be easily distinguished from the surrounding layers, since it tends to be darker and damper (as the humus retains moisture). Because the wood tends to rot from the top, the post-hole filling often becomes darker with depth, as the humus sinks and the upper part fills with earth. This is important, since post-holes may not always be seen at the original ground surface, but only picked up as the excavation proceeds downward. This, in turn, may lead to the post-hole being assumed to belong to a lower layer than it really does, so that it will then be assigned to an earlier period in the site's history.

3   It may be burnt. In this case, the rim of the post-hole will often be charred or burnt red. The stump of the post may have burnt freely in the open air, but below ground, where there is less air, it will tend to be turned to charcoal. This charcoal may well be datable by carbon-14 analysis (see the glossary).

4   The post may have been set in waterlogged ground, as in a marsh, or may have become waterlogged due to a rising water table. Sometimes only the bottom of the post, if it is set in stiff clay, for example, will be waterlogged. In all these cases, the timber will tend to be preserved, due to the fact that decay is inhibited by the lack of air. Clearly, waterlogged

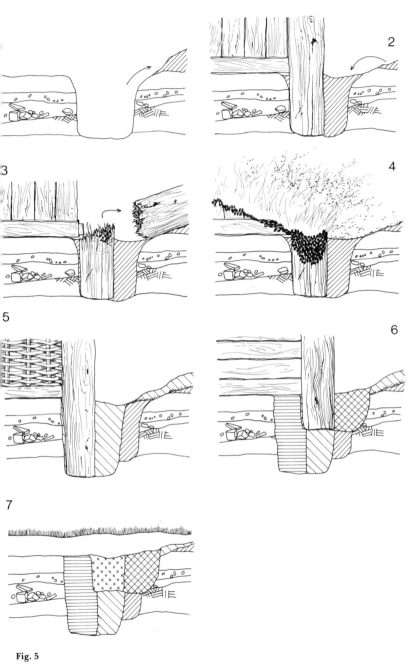

Fig. 5

Figs. 5 and **6** show some of the ways in which post-holes, as we find them on excavations, are formed. **Fig. 5** shows the post structures in section and **Fig. 6** shows the same features in plan.

In **5.1** a pit has been dug to take the post, and in **5.2** the post has been inserted as part of a building and the remainder of the pit back-filled. This is the way in which countless washing-line posts and telegraph poles have been erected.

In **5.3** it has been assumed that the post has rotted *in situ*. This rotting usually occurs at ground level, for the reasons outlined on p. 00.

6.3a shows the pit with the remains of the post in plan. This is one of the commonest features on sites which contained timber buildings. In **5.4** it is supposed that the building burnt down. In this case the top of the post-stub may be converted into charcoal. Sometimes the whole of the post-hole is full of charcoal; in other cases there will be only a trace around the edge of the post-hole which may be reddened or charred. The remains of the post which are left in the ground may be dug out so that the post can be replaced, or the post may simply be left to rot. In the latter case, the wood is eventually replaced by soil, due to the actions of micro-organisms, fungi and other agents of decay, and of earthworms and insects, which transport soil into the vacant spaces left by the rotting timber. If the ground is waterlogged, however, the remains of the post may be preserved, due to the fact that, under these conditions (which are known as *anaerobic*, because there is lack of air), micro-organisms and other agents of decay cannot exist, and so the decaying process is stopped or considerably retarded.

If the post-stub is dug out it usually happens that the new hole is not the same size as the first, and it then becomes clear, on excavation, that the hole has been re-dug (**5.5** and **5.6**). The process of renewing posts in the same place can be repeated many times – some hillfort gateways have had as many as fifteen replaced posts, detectable to the excavator because they have been replaced in slightly different positions each time.

5.7 shows a notional section of a series of post-holes and -pits which might be found if a post had been replaced twice. The plan view is seen in **6.7a**. It will be seen that, if the posts have been replaced many more times than this, a very complicated situation will be created in the ground – one which requires a great deal of skill in digging and interpretation.

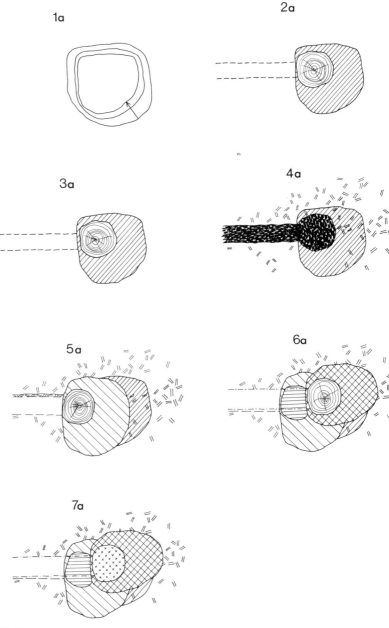

Fig. 6

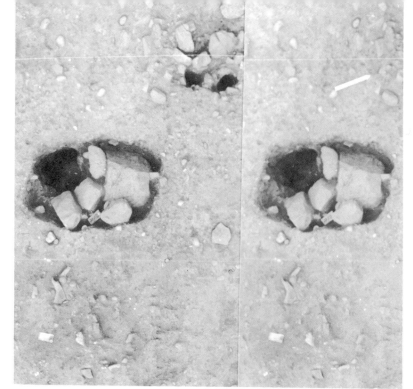

Fig. 7

Fig. 7 A vertical stereoscopic view of a post-hole. The post-pit, which is oval, can be seen packed with stones placed to support the round post which was placed in one corner of the pit. The post-pit is 70cm (28in) acrosss its greatest width and the post-hole (and therefore the post) is 20cm (8in) in diameter. This pair of pictures has been placed so that they can be viewed stereoscopically with a hand-viewer. (Photo: Sidney Renow)

Fig. 8 Most post-holes are formed by the posts rotting in their holes. **Figs. 8a, b and c** show two spectacular posts and the beginnings of their decline into nothing more than vegetable mould in two large holes in the ground. It will be appreciated how impossible it would be to imagine what the totems were like simply on the basis of their post-holes – a good example of the limitations of archaeological evidence.

The photographs of the totem poles were taken in 1901, 1948 and 1980 respectively. The poles belong to the Kunghit Haida people of Ninstits Village on Anthony Island in British Columbia. This is the largest and best preserved collection of *in situ* totem poles in the world. The two illustrated here are mortuary poles, with a niche for the remains of the deceased at the top. The village was abandoned in the 1880s and the age of the poles is thought to be between 130-140 years. They are situated on the shoreline, with a dense Sitka spruce forest behind them. Because of photographs taken from time to time by visitors (often on

Fig. 8a

the removal of some of the remaining poles to museums) the deterioration and eventual collapse of these fine wooden monuments can be monitored.

In the course of the years, the forest has moved forward to engulf the poles. In the niches of the graveposts, on exposed ledges of the sculptured surface and at the base of the poles, seeds, leaves and bird droppings accumulated and retained enough moisture to support the growth of plants, including seedling spruces, fungi and bacteria. Eventually it was the weight of the spruce trees growing in the mortuary niches which caused the poles to snap at ground level and to become uprooted, rather than decay at the base, though the humus and moisture on the poles has accelerated the decay of the wood by micro-organisms (fungi and bacteria). Shrubs and grasses growing at the bases of the poles have produced optimal conditions (moist and shade) for bacteria and soft rot fungi on the wood. Once a pole falls to the ground it rots very quickly.

Fig. 8a was taken in 1901, when the poles were probably only 30 or 40 years old. The carving on the nearest pole represents a killer whale and the protruding plank of wood is its dorsal fin. It can be seen that plants are already growing on the ledge of the mortuary niche.

Fig. 8b was taken in 1948. The dorsal fin has been lost. Sitka spruce are growing in both mortuary niches.

Fig. 8b

Fig. 8c

Fig. 8c was taken in 1971. Both poles have fallen. Eventually all that will be left will be two large post-holes.
(Photo: courtesy of the British Columbia Provincial Musuem, Victoria, British Columbia)

1

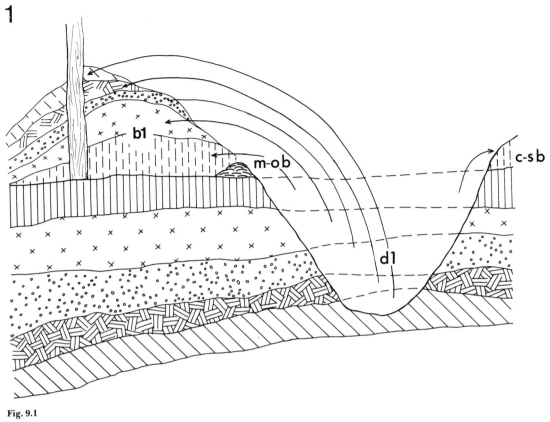

Fig. 9.1

2

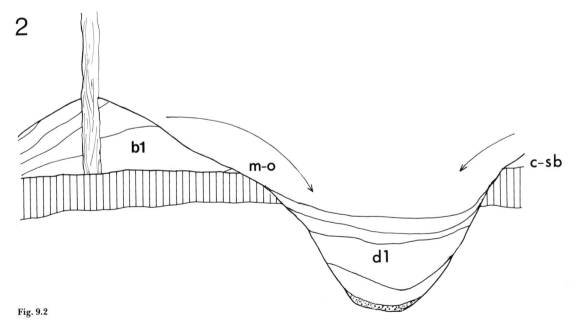

Fig. 9.2

Figs. 9.1-7 illustrate the digging and redigging of a typical bank and ditch. In **9.1** the ditch, d1 has been cut through five layers, the topsoil (vertically shaded) and four underlying layers of undisturbed subsoil. Part of the topsoil has been thrown up on the outside (the undefended side) of the ditch to form a small counterscarp bank, c-s b. Turf and topsoil have also been thrown up on the inside to form a marking-out bank, m-o b. These two slight banks mark out the size of the ditch to be dug by the ditch-digging labourers, who then throw the material up to form the bank. Though shown rather simplistically in the drawing, the layers will tend to be deposited on the bank in the reverse order from that in which they lay in the ground (reversed stratigraphy).

Immediately the bank has been formed it starts to erode. Loose material falls back into the ditch, followed by silts washed down by the first rains (the primary silting). Left to itself, the ditch gradually fills up, while the bank is denuded, and becomes lower and less steep-sided. The point may come where the bank and ditch have lost their defensive capability, and the ditch is then recut to deepen it while using the material to heighten or reinforce the bank (**9.3**). It very often happens that the recut is shallower than the original ditch. If this happens, the layers forming the earliest silting of the first ditch are preserved (d1 in **9.3**).

Bank 2 erodes in its turn, and fills the bottom of ditch 2 (**9.4**). This, in turn, may be recut, forming ditch and bank b3 (**9.5**). Bank 3 erodes in its turn and fills ditch d3 (**9.6**). Eventually, when the site is abandoned, the whole may be ploughed, but, nevertheless, under the ploughsoil, the evidence remains of the three ditches and, at least by

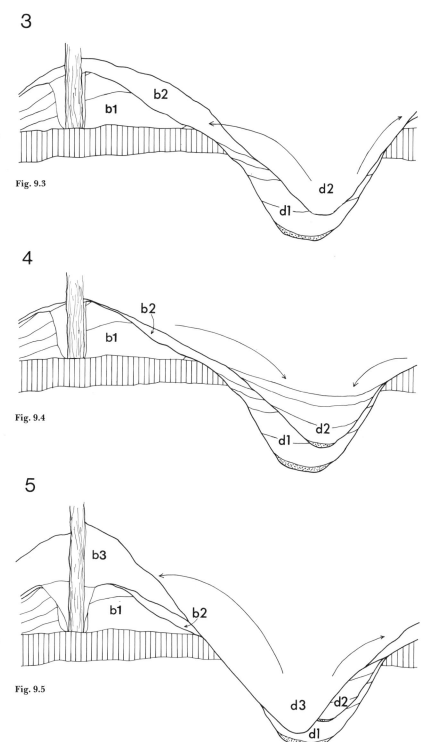

3

Fig. 9.3

4

Fig. 9.4

5

Fig. 9.5

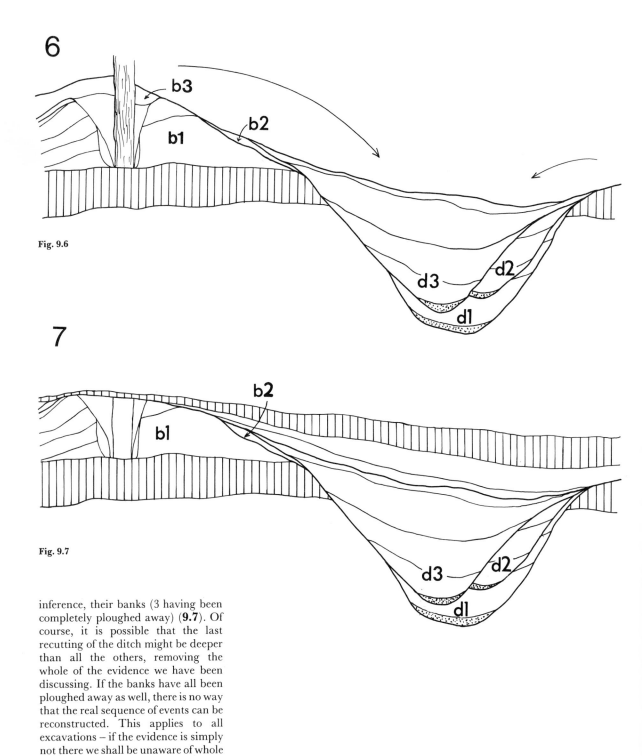

6

Fig. 9.6

7

Fig. 9.7

inference, their banks (3 having been completely ploughed away) (**9.7**). Of course, it is possible that the last recutting of the ditch might be deeper than all the others, removing the whole of the evidence we have been discussing. If the banks have all been ploughed away as well, there is no way that the real sequence of events can be reconstructed. This applies to all excavations – if the evidence is simply not there we shall be unaware of whole periods or phases in the life of the site.

sites provide tangible evidence of timber structures and help to interpret those sites where only ghosts of timbers, in the form of post-holes, are left.

A distinction must be made between the post-hole (or post-pipe) and the pit in which it is set – the post-pit. This is sometimes very difficult to distinguish in the ground, since the post-pit is often back-filled immediately with the material which has just been dug out of it. One of the skills which the excavator needs is to be able to distinguish between disturbed and undisturbed soil – to notice the way in which the stones in it lie, or the very slight changes in colour and texture brought about by the fact that disturbance loosens the structure of the soil and often makes it slightly darker, perhaps because it becomes mixed with small amounts of humus, perhaps because it is slightly more aerated, and the iron salts in it become oxidized. At Hen Domen, Montgomery, the undisturbed boulder clay is slightly paler and yellower, rather than ochrous, compared with the disturbed clay of post-pits (Barker and Higham, 1982). Sometimes the distinction between the post-pit and the subsoil can only be felt with the trowel, where, though the difference is not visible, the texture changes and can be detected.

Sometimes it is possible to distinguish between two or more groups of post-holes on the basis of their filling. To take a simple example – the post-pits belonging to the first buildings put up on the site will be filled with clean earth; a subsequent building's post-pits will contain a proportion of recognizable debris from the occupation which preceded their digging. (See a good example from the excavation at Yeavering – Hope-Taylor, 1977, Fig.10 and pp.42-45.)

DITCHES

Defensive ditches and drainage ditches are very common on sites of all kinds and periods, and some general rules apply to their understanding. To take defensive ditches first – the spoil from the ditch digging is usually thrown up on the inside to form a rampart if the ditch surrounds the site, or on the side to be defended if the ditch is linear, like Wansdyke or Offa's Dyke. Most dry ditches are V-shaped, though ditches which are intended to be water-filled, such as those around moated sites, are usually flat-bottomed. The ditch starts to silt up almost as soon as it is dug. The first shower of rain will erode the sides and bring down fine runnels of soil to the bottom, and, more importantly, the loose earth and stones on the edge of the new rampart will fall back into the ditch. This earliest filling is known as the 'primary silt' (Fig. 9.2). Thereafter, the silting of the ditch will depend on a number of factors: the soil in which the ditch has been cut (there will clearly be a great difference between the speed of silting of a ditch cut in sand and one cut in boulder clay); the steepness of the original sides; the rapidity with which the surfaces are consolidated with vegetation and whether the ditch is dry or waterlogged.

If the ditch is accompanied by a bank or rampart, it follows that there will be more silting on the rampart side than on the open side (see Figs. 9.2/3/4). Even in cases where the rampart has been completely ploughed away, it is nevertheless often possible to postulate its former existence by the greater quantity of silting on one side (Fig. 9.7).

To the natural erosion of the banks and the silting of the ditch must be added the accidental filling which will occur if the defensive site is slighted or destroyed, when rampart material is likely to collapse into the ditch. Sometimes, also, ditches are filled deliberately, either to deny their use to an enemy (a common practice in Roman times) or to bring an abandoned site back into agricultural use. It is usually, though not always, possible to tell whether a layer has been thrown into the ditch deliberately or has silted naturally due to weathering – the deliberate filling is likely to be in the form of clods or unsorted stones, though here again, if the ditch is filled in dry weather, the stones contained in the soil will sort themselves naturally on the way down, as any one who has every back-filled a hole will know.

The 'reading' of ditch sections is, however, complicated by the fact that ditches are very often recut, sometimes almost to their original depth, at other times quite shallowly, in order to maintain their defensive effectiveness. When this has happened, the recuts can usually be distinguished by the fact that they cut across the lines of the normal silting and filling. Figs. 9.1-7 illustrate this.

Drainage ditches are, by definition, meant to carry water, and so they will silt up due to material carried down after rain, both from their sides and along their length. One effect of this is that small objects may be carried a considerable distance down the drain, far from the place in' which they were dropped, so that deductions about the buildings or settlements near the ditch may be mistaken.

Ramparts
Ramparts are usually formed from the spoil upcast from the ditch which goes with them. In many cases, therefore, the size of the rampart is determined by the size of the ditch. Since, except in the case of linear earthworks, such as Offa's Dyke, defensive ditches are used to form enclosures, the circumference of the rampart inside the ditch will be a good deal less than that of the ditch itself, so that the rampart can be correspondingly higher than the depth of the ditch.

From the archaeological point of view, the layers within a rampart will tend to be inverted from those that the ditch has been dug through. Often, the topsoil or ploughsoil will have been stripped off and placed on the surface of the topsoil along the line of the intended rampart, to form a marking-out bank. As the ditch-diggers dig through the layers of sub-soil they will throw them up on top of one another (Fig. 9.1). Things are

[*45*

Fig. 10. 1-4, shows the stages by which a wall may first be robbed of its visible stone and then the wall base and its foundations dug out, leaving a rubble-filled trench which, when ploughed over, cannot be seen on the surface.

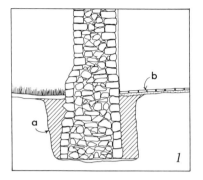
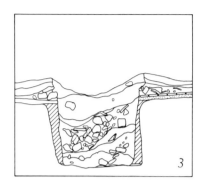
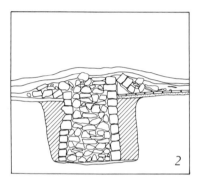
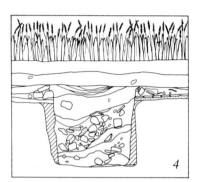

Fig. 10

Fig. 11 View along the robber trench of the south colonnade of the Baths Basilica at Wroxeter. The massive stylobate (foundation) stones for the columns have been robbed out, many of them for the building of Anglo-Saxon churches in the neighbourhood. The underlying footings, which can be seen in the picture, have been left in place – only the large worked blocks have been taken. The south wall of the basilica, seen on the left of the picture, has also been left. This is a good example of selective robbing, where only the stones which had a specific use were taken.

Fig. 11

Fig. 12

Variety of archaeological sites

Fig. 12 This is the centre of the Romano-British city at Wroxeter, *Viroconium Cornoviorum*. The view is of the public baths, with the Old Work, a massive fragment of the party wall between the baths and the basilica which formed a vast entrance hall to the bath complex. In many ways, it is the classical archaeological site – a ruin, parts of which still stand after more than 1800 years, laid out by the Department of the Environment with gravel paths and shaven grass. Yet this is only a tiny, visible, fraction of the whole city and its suburbs (see **Figs. 30a-c)** and even this part is imperfectly understood, in spite of the fact that it has been dug intermittently since the middle of the nineteenth century. The earliest excavations were, understandably, relatively crude and summary, removing much vital evidence unrecorded, particularly that relating to the later occupation of the site. This has made subsequent excavations all the more difficult because so much is missing.

Wroxeter is, of course, only one of many Roman towns in Britain; a considerable proportion lie under present towns – London, Lincoln, Gloucester and York are well-known examples. A few, such as Wroxeter, Verulamium (St Albans), Silchester and Caerwent have no later settlements of any size on them and these are the sites which will, it is hoped, be fully explored and displayed in the future.

Fig. 13

Fig. 13 Some of the largest and most spectacular excavations of the last ten years have been carried out in advance of development in cities. Urban archaeology on this scale has particular problems – it is always rescue excavation, since no urban site is available indefinitely; the stratification is usually very deep, so that the excavation is not only complex, but requires a high level of civil engineering in order to render it safe. It is also very expensive – land values, and the cost of development verge on the astronomic, and therefore time also is expensive. Intensive excavation on this scale demands a high degree of organisation – much of the effort has to go into fund-raising, administration and liaison with the city councils, developers and architects responsible. On the other hand, not only are the results of such concentrated excavation highly rewarding in terms of their results, but they also provide an unrivalled opportunity to explain not only the excavation, but archaeology generally, to the large numbers of people who pass the site.

Here, in the early stages of the excavations of a site at Billingsgate, in the City of London, the archaeologists are dealing with the medieval levels of the site while public viewing platforms are being erected on the street frontage.

(Photo: courtesy of the Museum of London)

Fig. 14

Fig. 15

Fig. 14 A great building such as a cathedral, with an immensely long history, has much of this history embedded within its standing structure, and, over the last century, architectural historians have spent a great deal of time and thought on the elucidation of the development of cathedrals and churches. But much of the evidence lies below ground, so that study of the architecture and excavation must go hand in hand.

Fig. 14 shows the excavation of one of the piers of the central tower of the cathedral at Worcester. The excavation was carried out to examine the foundations which, as can be seen, consist of a massive cross-shaped block of masonry, A, which dates from 1084. As can also be seen, the present tower, B, built in the later part of the fourteenth century, is diamond-shaped rather than square in plan. The excavation showed clearly that a second tower had been built between the collapse of the first in 1175 and the building of the present tower (see Barker 1982, Figs. 14a and b).

Excavations within a building of this kind which is constantly in use have to be restricted to the smallest effective area, and carried out as quickly as possible, in order not to disrupt the work of the cathedral more than is absolutely necessary.

(Photo: author)

Fig. 15 Castles: very many early castles were of timber on massive earthworks (see Figs. 29a and 42) but they were built, or rebuilt, increasingly in stone from the twelfth century onward.

This is the castle at Clun, in Shropshire, built originally in timber, with a very large motte, or mound. This castle was burnt by the Welsh towards the end of the twelfth century, and the keep, seen here, was rebuilt in stone in a style transitional between Norman and Early English. Because the builders were not sure of the stability of the artificial mound, they built the keep in its side, driving the foundations down to the solid rock. Nevertheless, the motte is covered with less massive stone buildings now reduced to rubble and earthworks. On the opposite side of the little River Clun is a square moated site which is, in fact, the remains of a *pleasaunce* or formal garden for the ladies of the castle.

See p. 99-100 for excavation of a stone castle.

Fig. 16

Fig. 17

Fig. 16 Linear earthworks: this is a stretch of Offa's Dyke near Montgomery, Powys, which, together with a shorter dyke known as Wat's Dyke (both dating from the eighth century) snakes for some 156 miles along the English-Welsh border 'from sea to sea' – from Chepstow to Prestatyn. Both are typical of frontier dykes dating from prehistoric times onward. Many of these great earthworks have been obliterated or badly damaged and often only their filled-in ditches are left, to be discovered by excavation. One of the unsolved problems of Offa's Dyke is whether or not there was a palisade with fighting platform on its crest. This is a problem which can only be solved by excavation, but, curiously, none has been carried out, and there are now only a few stretches, such as this one, in which the evidence may still survive, and these stretches are being continually eroded by walkers on the Offa's Dyke path, not to mention the cows. This is typical of the dilemma caused by the very great increase in tourism which is threatening the very monuments which visitors come to see. (Photo: author)

Fig. 17 Two for the price of one . . . This is a photograph of British Camp, Malvern, Worcestershire, a massive hillfort with a central 'citadel' with extensions on both sides. It is pock-marked with shallow pits or platforms. These have been thought to be house-sites, though some archaeologists have suggested that they are natural hollows in the rock surface. The large ditched mound at the summit of the hill has been shown by excavation to be a Norman motte, or castle mound. Such castles, which date from the century after the Norman Conquest are usually found in or near to settlements. This at the remote top of a hill, may be a fortified hunting-lodge – Malvern Chase was a famous and extensive hunting-ground. The tracks show the damage caused to monuments by a constant stream of visitors. (Photo: Arnold Baker)

Fig. 18

Figs. 18 and 19 These two aerial photographs are both of ditched enclosures. Fig. 18 is of a medieval moated site in Warwickshire, surviving, as so many moated sites do, as a prominent earthwork. Fig. 19 is also in Warwickshire, but is of a double-ditched enclosure, larger than that in Fig. 18, and now ploughed completely flat. It is probably pre-historic since it is overlain with medieval ridge and furrow cultivation. Both sites are, nevertheless, related in type, since both very probably enclosed one or more house sites.
(Photos: Arnold Baker)

Fig. 19

Fig. 20 Aerial photograph of the Roman fort at Wall-town, Cleobury Mortimer, Shropshire. The left-hand half of the fort is preserved as an unpstanding earthwork, A, but the right-hand half, on the other side of the road, shows up only as a crop-mark, B, in the field of cereal. Although the building of the farm has destroyed much of the fort, it is probably the presence of the buildings that has preserved the ramparts, which would long ago have been ploughed away if they had been out in the open fields. (Photo: Arnold Baker)

Fig. 20

Fig. 21 Ring-ditches showing up as crop-marks (see the glossary) in modern cultivation. The nearest, largest, of the rings, A, is probably a henge monument with two entrances, a 'temple' site akin to Stonehenge and Avebury, though much smaller. (Photo: Arnold Baker)

Fig. 21

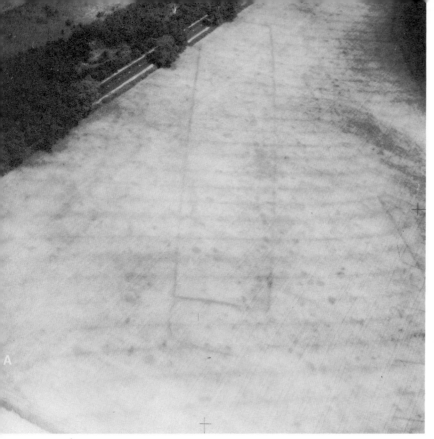

Fig. 22

Fig. 22 This photograph shows the crop-mark of the ditches of a large cursus, thought to be a ritual enclosure of neolithic date. The hook-shaped feature at the end of the enclosure is probably contemporary; the dark spots may be storage pits, while in the bottom left-hand corner is part of a pit-alignment, A, a form of early boundary. The whole area is covered with the curving lines of ploughed-out ridge and furrow of a medieval field. An idea of the size of this beautifully laid out monument can be gauged from the 'A' road in the background. The whole site has now been destroyed by gravel extraction.
(Photo: Arnold Baker)

Fig. 23

Fig. 23 Crop-marks of a very complex site in Warwickshire. A wide trackway, A, runs through the whole site and divides into two in the upper part of the picture. Another, even wider, track, B, joins the first from the right and continues, less clearly, out of the picture to the left. The whole field in the foreground is full of enclosures, some no doubt for stock, others enclosing house-sites. It is also clear that the settlement spans many periods of occupation, since many of the features overlap, so cannot be contemporary. The settlement probably spans the Bronze and Iron Ages in date, though only excavation would confirm this.
(Photo: Arnold Baker)

Fig. 24

Fig. 24 Crop-marks of a group of Anglo-Saxon halls at Hatton Rock in Warwickshire. Large rectangular buildings in line are characteristic of Saxon halls or 'palaces' – these have been firmly dated by Philip Rahtz, who recovered Anglo-Saxon pottery from a pipe trench dug across the site by the owner. The building with the curved (apsidal) end near the upper edge of the photograph, A, may be a church. The significance of some of the other crop-marks is not clear, and they may well date from an entirely different period.
(Photo: Arnold Baker)

Fig. 25a

Figs. 25a-g These illustrations are of an Iron Age and Romano-British enclosed settlement at Collfryn, Powys, excavated by the Clwyd-Powys Archaeological Trust. **Figs. 25a** and **b** are aerial photographs of the double-ditched enclosure which lies on a low ridge some 6 miles north of Welshpool. Half the site (B on both figures) is still an earthwork, though much eroded. The other half (A) can be seen as a soil-mark, or, in the growing season, a crop-mark. The white streaks in **Fig. 25b** are caused by melting snow left in slight hollows in the ground. The site was excavated because of continued erosion by ploughing, and because settlements of this kind are virtually unexplored. As can be seen from **Figs. 25f** and **g**, the surface evidence gives no hint of the complexity of the occupation of the interior, and, of course, there is no way of dating the occupation or assessing its length without excavation.
(Photo: Chris Musson)

Fig. 25b

Fig. 25g is a plan of all the excavated structures and features, chiefly round-houses of Iron Age date. **Fig. 25c** is of the entrance; **Fig. 25e** is a photograph of the house at C on **Fig. 25d**, occupied from about 300 BC until the later part of the first century BC, just before the Roman Conquest. The large rectangular subdivisions of the interior appear to date from Roman times, between the second and fourth centuries AD, suggesting that the enclosure was reused for perhaps some agricultural purpose. The corn-drying kiln, marked on **Fig. 25g**, has now been dated to the mid-fifteenth century AD by radio-carbon examination of charcoal from the stokehole. Such kilns are well-attested in Welsh documents.

(Plans and photos: kind permission of the Clwyd-Powys Trust, and in particular Jenny and Bill Britnell)

Fig. 25d

Fig. 25e

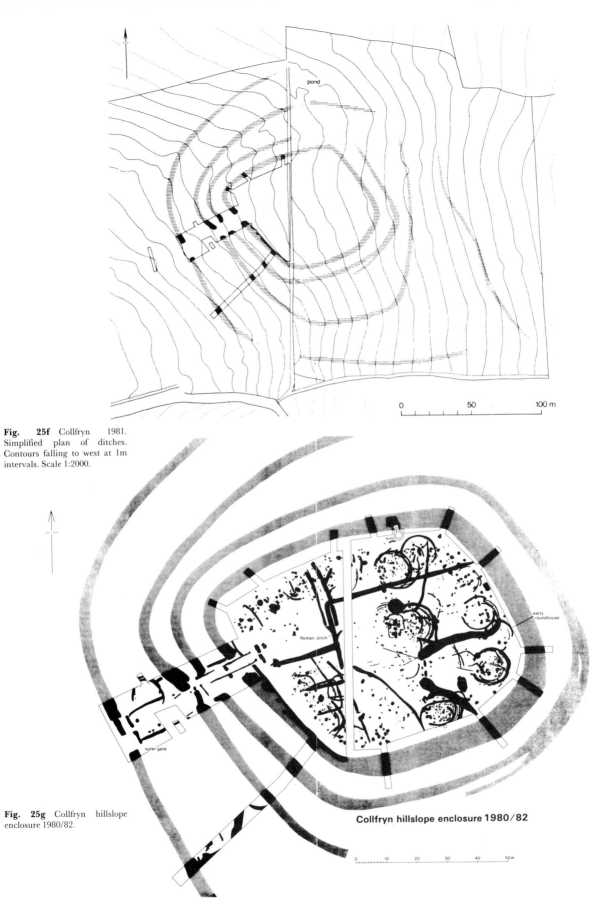

Fig. 25f Collfryn 1981. Simplified plan of ditches. Contours falling to west at 1m intervals. Scale 1:2000.

Fig. 25g Collfryn hillslope enclosure 1980/82.

pond

0   50   100 m

kiln

early
roundhouse

Roman ditch

outer gate

Collfryn hillslope enclosure 1980/82

0   10   20   30   40   50m

Figs. 26a-d Probably the largest archaeological sites in Britain or Europe are the prehistoric landscapes, now almost entirely reduced to crop-mark sites, revealed by aerial photography, particularly in the great river valleys. Some of these sites stretch for miles, covering many hundreds of acres with intensive occupation (**Fig. 26c**). **Fig. 26a** is a photograph of part of one, at Beckford, in the valley of the Avon in Worcestershire. This site, which, like so many others of its kind, has been completely removed by gravel extraction, has been excavated by the Hereford and Worcester Archaeology Department, directed by Jan Wills. **Fig. 26b** shows the method of excavation. As wide strips of the site became available (the excavations were sandwiched between the quarry on one side and a blackcurrant orchard on the other) they were excavated by hand after the machine removal of the immediate topsoil. The site consisted of a mass of enclosures, some for stock, others containing houses. The area excavated is shown on **Fig. 26c** and is also contained within the aerial photograph. The enclosures marked A, B and C can be seen on both, but the interim plan, **Fig. 26d**, shows clearly how much more was revealed by the excavation. Not only were the enclosures much more complex and of many more periods of occupation and renewal than appears on the photograph, but there is also a multitude of storage and rubbish pits, and many house sites.

In many ways this settlement is typical of those on the sands and gravels of the river valleys. It was occupied from the early Iron Age up to Roman times, though a little further down the valley occupation continues into the Anglo-

Fig. 26a

Saxon period. This intensity of prehistoric occupation, spread over such a large area, was hardly suspected until aerial photography revealed it, mainly after the Second World War.

Fig. 26c is a plot of crop-marks in part of the Avon valley in Worcestershire. The Carrant Brook is a tributary of the Avon. The Beckford site is marked A on the map. The sites marked 13 and 14 are part of the catalogue of sites published by Graham Webster and Brian Hobley in *The Archaeological Journal*, Vol. 121 (1964), 1-22, from which this map is taken.

Fig. 26d is a plan of part of the excavation at Beckford.

(Photo: Arnold Baker. Drawings: courtesy of [jd?], Jan Wills and Brian Hobley)

Fig. 26b

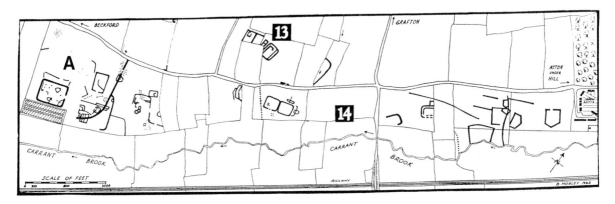

Fig. 26c

BECKFORD 1972-79

0   50m

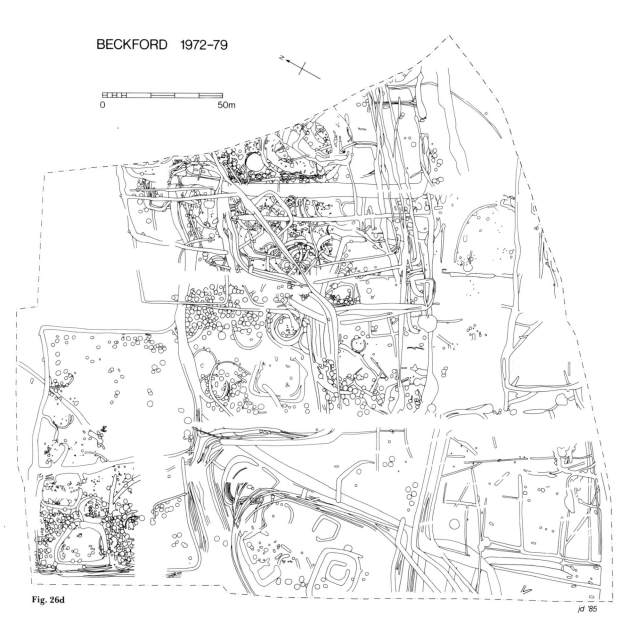

Fig. 26d

jd '85

Fig. 27

Fig. 27 *Wetland sites*
If organic materials, such as wood, leather, plants and seeds are kept continuously wet from the time of their deposition in the ground until they are dug up, they remain remarkably preserved. As a result, sites in fens, marshes, lakes and, of course, in the case of ships, the sea, are likely to produce far more evidence, not only of structures but also of finds which would otherwise have disappeared. This illustration shows a waterlogged site in Cambridgeshire – Flag Fen, near Peterborough, under excavation by Francis Pryor and Maisie Taylor. Among the mass of timbers which are strewn over the whole site are some which are still embedded in their original positions, though rotted off where they have protruded above the level which has been continuously wet. The whole site is kept damp with agricultural sprays and by covering the parts not being worked on with polythene sheet to retain the moisture. Recording on such a site presents particular difficulties as the timbers not only project above the surface but do so at all angles. The timbers lying between the uprights also have to be recorded in detail, since their positions reflect the way in which the structures have collapsed, or been demolished.
The site dates from the Late Bronze or Early Iron Age, *c.* 660 BC and is being dug in advance of drainage, which, by drying out the site, would cause the timbers eventually to rot away.
It is instructive to compare this site with that at Beckford (Figs. 26a-d) which is in many ways similar, though, because it is well-drained on gravel, has lost its timbers and other organic finds.
(Photo: courtesy of Francis Pryor)

rarely as simple as that, of course; for example, the sequence may be complicated by the fact that the palisade and rampart are built simultaneously, the rampart material being piled round the palisade posts from the ground up.

Sometimes it is possible to detect gang-work in the building of ramparts, where different lengths are built separately, as Sir Cyril Fox suggested in the construction of Offa's Dyke (Fox, 1955, 80, 121-22, 153, etc.). At Hen Domen, Montgomery, it was possible to see that the rampart had been piled from west to east in overlapping mounds of clay (Barker and Higham, 1982, Fig. 17, section g-e).

MOUNDS

The construction of mounds may vary from a motte or barrow of simple dump construction to a highly complex series of superimposed occupation deposits, as found, for instance, in the *terpen* of Holland and north Germany or, at the far end of the scale, the *tells* of the Middle East, which contain the remains of whole cities. Generalizations are not, therefore, very helpful. Yet more mounds of various sorts have been dug, and dug badly, than perhaps any other sort of monument, since they are not only obvious, but they seem to be self-contained, to have edges, and therefore to be suitable for limited excavation. It is not surprising that one of the earliest published archaeological sections (in colour!) is that which Thomas Jefferson cut across an Indian burial mound in 1784 (Sherratt, ed., 1980, 15).

STONE ROBBING AND ROBBER TRENCHES

The quarrying of stone is very laborious and costly, especially if it entails transporting it over long distances. As a result, stone is reused whenever possible, often many times. A late Roman tombstone from Wroxeter, for instance, had started life as a tombstone, probably in the first century, had subsequently been cut down and used as a building stone, when it had been exposed to considerable wear on one of its faces, and was then, perhaps as late as the mid-fifth century, again used as a tombstone. Churches, either in part or entire, were constantly being knocked down and their stone reused, often simply as rubble. The two well-attested Anglo-Saxon Minsters at Worcester, one dating from the seventh century and the other from the tenth and both still in existence just before the Norman Conquest, have disappeared completely, absorbed, presumably, in the fabric of the cathedral begun by St Wulstan in 1084. The parish churches of Wroxeter, Atcham and Upton Magna, all near the Roman town of *Viroconium Cornoviorum*, are built very largely of stone from the buildings of the Roman town (Figs. 11 and 12), as are farm buildings and walls for miles around. These examples can, of course, be paralleled all over the world where stone is the principal building material.

Not only do masons knock down buildings to reuse the stone, but they dig out the foundations of demolished buildings to recover the stone, which may only be rubble. The trenches thus left, usually back-filled with the unusable mortar and stone debris, are termed *robber trenches* (see the glossary) and are very often the only evidence for former buildings.

THE VARIETY OF ARCHAEOLOGICAL SITES

One of the problems in understanding excavation lies in the immense variety of archaeological sites, which range from single house-steads to whole cities and from burial mounds to cathedrals. They range in time from the earliest hominid occupation sites some three million years old, to industrial sites of the last 50 years; in fact to many of us 'archaeology began yesterday'.

Figs. 12-27 show something of this variety and illustrate the difficulty of generalising about excavation. Are there any general principles which govern the excavations of a rock shelter on the one hand and the deeply stratified centre of a modern city on the other? We shall attempt to answer this question in Chapter 4.

CHAPTER TWO

The development of techniques

WHERE TO DIG?

The reasons for embarking on an excavation have changed radically over the last 50 years – in fact, they have changed dramatically over the last 15 years. In the 1930s excavations were dictated by either the research interests of the excavator, or the curiosity of amateurs – a form of local history. These attitudes persisted through the period of the Second World War up till the 1950s. Though there had been efforts, notably by the Council for British Archaeology, to co-ordinate field-work and excavation, and archaeology had gradually become a more respectable subject in the universities, there was little real organization, and the Inspectorate of Ancient Monuments financed excavation on a very small scale. In 1939, when the Sutton Hoo Ship Burial was excavated, the Ministry of Works' contribution was, by present-day standards, derisory, and, as late as the 1950s, directors of rescue excavations funded by the Ministry of Works were expected to write up their excavations in their own time. This led not only to long delays or non-publication, but, in some cases, to real hardship.

It was probably the realization of the true losses of archaeological evidence caused by developments of all kinds, but particularly urban renewal, motorway construction and sand and gravel quarrying, that led to the spectacular increase in finance, and consequently in excavation, in advance of the destruction of sites. But this was rescue and salvage excavation; in other words, the choice of site was dictated by the developer or the line of a motorway, not by archaeological considerations. There was a tendency in the 1970s to try to dig everything, or at least to try to salvage something from every potential loss. Any evidence which could be recovered seemed better than nothing. This is now seen as a fallacy – see Chapter 4.

There was some attempt to co-ordinate work on groups of sites, to develop rescue excavation as a form of research, to get away from the 'single site syndrome', as Peter Fowler called it, and to study whole landscapes, both rural and urban, in their contexts; but the sites of by far the greatest number of excavations were chosen by developers and not by archaeologists – 'fire-brigade' archaeology, as it has been called, with teams of diggers leaping into the field as the alarm bells rang. There were also 'research excavations', that is, excavations being carried out on sites which were not threatened, except by archaeologists; and since, as we have said, all excavation is destruction, a site destroyed by archaeological excavation, however skilled, is as effectively destroyed as by a bull-dozer.

Thus we have a major ethical dilemma. There is a clear case to be made for the excavation of a site in advance of its obliteration if that obliteration is inevitable. Can, however, a case be made for the archaeological destruction of a site as a piece of research, when we remember that the number of sites is diminishing rapidly – a 'wasting asset' if ever there was one. What arguments can we use to justify digging a site now, in the name of curiosity (if you wish, the higher curiosity which we call research) and not leaving it for the future, for someone else to destroy who might be able to extract far more information from it than we can with our presumably more primitive methods?

Twenty years ago, there did not seem to be a problem: sites were there to be dug. Now we see them as a precious and dwindling asset, to be preserved, so far as is possible. Should only those sites which are about to be destroyed or deeply damaged be excavated (bearing in mind that we have no chance of excavating even a hundredth of the sites which are being destroyed or damaged annually)? Isn't rescue excavation enough to satisfy our need for information, without our turning to unthreatened sites? The dilemma is made greater because we now realize that the method used extensively in the past, of digging a small part of a site and assuming it to represent the whole, is almost always highly misleading. Research excavation on an unthreatened site requires, therefore, the destruction of a large part of that site, and it implies arrogance on the part of the director to believe that he (or she) should destroy it now and not leave it for another 100 or 200 years. One of the most trenchant critics of the extensive excavation of unthreatened sites is Professor Olaf Olsen (see Chapter 4).

The consciousness of the dilemma between the fact that total excavation is totally destructive, but that limited excavation produces results which may be misleading, and will certainly be, in some respect or other, unsatisfactory, has led to a greater sense of responsibility in the choice of sites to be excavated, and a shift from excavation towards preservation of sites where this is at all possible. This change in attitude is reminiscent of a similar, though much earlier, change in the attitude of naturalists from 'If you don't know what it is, shoot it' to the present conservation legislation which prosecutes you if you attempt to sell a collection of bird's eggs left to you by your granny.

As a result of this shift of opinion, much more thought is being given to the reasons for digging at all, and to which of the available sites should be dug.

The factors to be taken into account fall into a number of categories: first, the profusion, rarity or even uniqueness of the type of site. Clearly the site thought to be unique will have a high priority for preservation at all costs. Stonehenge is the classic example, and there would now have to be very persuasive arguments for further excavation there. Other sorts of site are considered rare, and these might include the sites of Anglo-Saxon halls of the type excavated at Yeavering, or what is left of the centres of our medieval cities. Yet other categories of site are, by comparison, common – for example, there are some 2000 ring-forts of earth or stone in Ireland and over 2000 deserted medieval village sites in England. It might be thought that with such profusion a few would not be missed, but the problem is considerably compounded by the fact that, when these sites are excavated, no two are found to be the same, and it is certainly not possible to generalize from the few that have been excavated about the 200 or 2000 that have not. The loss of each one is, in some sense, a unique loss; nevertheless, it must be argued that the loss of 0.01 per cent of such sites is preferable to the loss of 10 per cent of a much rarer category.

Another factor which must be taken into account is the quality of the evidence which is predicted from the site. For example, a site discovered by aerial photography from crop-marks in a field which has been ploughed for centuries can be assumed to be damaged to a greater or lesser degree; it may have lost all, or most, of its stratified occupation deposits, and all that may be left are the deeper ditches and gullies and the bottoms of post-holes. In addition, the acidity of the soil may have destroyed all the organic remains, including bone, and severely corroded any metalwork. By contrast, in a site which has been continuously waterlogged, such as a crannog (see the glossary), or the deeper levels of low-lying cities, such as Dublin, York, Carlisle, or Novgorod, the preservation of structures, of finds of all kinds, and environmental evidence such as insects and seeds may be little short of miraculous. The same is true of sites which have remained totally dry in, for example, deserts, or been deep-frozen in perma-frost, such as the Scythian tombs at Pazyryk in Siberia, or the recently discovered Eskimo burials in Greenland. There are, of course, many less extreme cases, in which the degree of preservation may be partial, or the depth of the occupation deposits considerable, though without any preservation of organic remains.

This leads to the crucial problem of site evaluation – the non-destructive assessment of the site's archaeological potential before decisions are made whether or not to dig. The methods of doing this are discussed in Chapter 3. One cannot, however, take the simple view that all waterlogged sites, since they preserve more evidence, should take priority over 'dry' sites, because, for one thing, waterlogged sites are often fundamentally different in their types of structure, simply because they were built on low-lying or marshy ground. The buildings may be constructed on piles driven into the soft ground, or on rafts of logs or brushwood. The economy of such a settlement may rely, for obvious reasons, on fishing, or river or maritime trading. A settlement of the same size and date in hill country will have a different economy and different methods of building, so that it will be of equal interest, though unlikely to produce the wealth of evidence that the waterlogged site does.

Similarly, deeply-stratified unploughed sites may be thought to have precedence over thinly stratified ones; but, by this argument, whole categories of hill-top and moorland sites will find themselves downgraded compared with lowland sites, though the two are not really comparable, and need equal study.

Another factor which is less tangible but has a powerful influence is current fashion in research. In post-war Britain, Roman archaeology was predominant, perhaps because the methods of excavation then fashionable – the digging of trenches and boxes – proved more rewarding for the discovery and understanding of stone buildings than for the examination of the earthworks of prehistoric sites, medieval villages or motte and bailey castles. The latter, in particular, had always proved to be very resistant to trenching, producing time after time almost no evidence of any kind for the structures of the castle. Interest gradually swung towards the Dark Ages – the period between the end of Roman rule and the establishment of the Anglo-Saxon kingdoms, to prehistoric settlement sites of all periods and to the peasant houses which made up medieval villages, in spite of the fact that, as late as the 1960s, some distinguished antiquarians did not consider the 'huts and pigstyes of the peasantry' worthy of research at all.

There is no doubt that sites containing many superimposed periods of occupation do pose a real dilemma for the excavator, particularly when the site is threatened and time and resources are short. Ideally, every period from the recently demolished 1920s church hall to the deeply underlying prehistoric ditch system should be given the same meticulous treatment; but it almost never is, partly because there are few archaeologists who can raise equal enthusiasm for the nineteenth century BC and the nineteenth century AD together with everything in between, but, more often, because there are almost always strict limits to the time and money available. Not everything can be dug, and some parts of the site must therefore be given summary treatment or simply abandoned. It has happened, only too often, that excavations have begun with the best of intentions to dig the whole site in detail, but it is very easy, if you start by giving the full treatment to the uppermost levels of occupation, to run out of time and to have to leave the site just as rich and exciting levels, many metres below the surface, are emerging. Under these circumstances, hard decisions have to be taken: what should be sacrificed, or what should have been sacrificed? This question brings us back to the necessity of establishing, as far as is possible, the depth and complexity of the stratification, and how difficult it is likely to be to dig.

Intensive non-destructive prior examination of the site is of crucial importance here. For example, if there is every reason to believe that, sandwiched between the modern levels and the known Roman occupation, lies an intensively used cemetery of post-medieval date, then it must be realized that burials take a lot of very careful, time-consuming cleaning and recording and that that part of the excavation is likely to be very slow, so that greater allowance of time must be made for it. Alternatively, a positive decision must be made to sacrifice much of the information from the cemetery in order to get at the Roman occupation in time, and to gamble that the cemetery, seen in passing, as it were, does not prove to be much more interesting than what eventually turns out to be a more or less stereotyped Roman building with little new to offer. Nevertheless, cutting corners on excavations nearly always proves to be a mistake, so that I believe it is essential to speed up the processes of excavation and recording, using every technological advance that can be acquired (or afforded) so that the losses of evidence are reduced to a minimum.

All excavations face a number of common problems. First, they are chronologically upside-down, given that we always have to dig backwards through time, from the latest layers, the latest phases, of the site's occupation down to the earliest, which may lie many metres below the surface. The site's development is therefore revealed to us in reverse, so that, for instance, we see layers of destruction, rubble and debris before we see what it is that has been destroyed, or the progressive filling of a ditch before the ditch itself. To a large extent, therefore, we are always working into the unknown – we do not know the depth or character of a pit before we have emptied it, or the number of floors in a building from the vestiges of the latest. The upper surfaces of features are often extraordinarily misleading – a patch of burning may hide a carefully constructed hearth or simply fade out after a centimetre or so has been trowelled away. Not every patch of dark damp earth heralds a post-hole and massive building foundations may lie under tenuous lines of powdered mortar.

One of the most important and urgent needs of the excavator, therefore, is the development of non-destructive methods of pre-excavation survey, of ways of detecting buried features of all kinds before digging begins, and this problem will be discussed in Chapter 4.

Because we are always trowelling into the unknown we must continually be prepared for the unexpected, to dig with an open mind, and not dig to find what we want to find. Nevertheless, it is impossible to dig with a completely open mind – a blank sheet on which anything that turns up is simply recorded – since every excavation begins with a purpose, a problem or a series of problems to be solved. The crucial condition is that, on the one hand, the solving of a particular problem must not lead to an inflexible strategy which misses or ignores evidence of phases, periods or structures which are unexpected or do not fit in with the pre-conceived theories on which the excavation was based, and, on the other hand, whatever evidence is found must not be bent, even unconsciously, to support those pre-conceptions.

Perhaps the most flagrant examples of narrow problem-solving were those excavations in which the uppermost layers were bull-dozed off to get at the evidence for Roman occupation, whether in towns or in the countryside. The probability of evidence of later sub-Roman or post-Roman occupation of the greatest importance to our understanding of these obscure times seems to have been ignored or dismissed as irrelevant to an over-riding interest in the first to fourth centuries AD. Unbelievably, in the light of all that has been demonstrated to survive of the immediate post-Roman periods, this is still happening. In other cases, where the chief interest has shifted to, say, the Anglo-Saxon phases of a town, a deliberate decision has been made to strip off the later post-medieval and medieval deposits, on the grounds that what we need to know about *now* is the Anglo-Saxon development. It is argued that, while it would be desirable to excavate the whole sequence from top to bottom with the same attention to detail, the considerable extra expenditure in money and labour would not be justified. This argument is a powerful one when it is remembered that the vast majority of excavations are rescue excavations, and that public (and private) monies are strictly limited.

What part of the occupation sequence should be given summary treatment, or even entirely lost, in order to deal adequately with those periods which are considered to be more important, either in the history of a city, or in the light of the present state of knowledge or simply in the research interests of an individual? Many excavators argue that every period, every phase of the site's occupation, should be adequately dealt with and that, since the past is an unbroken whole up to the present, there is no excuse for summary treatment of any part of it. Unfortunately, it has happened more than once that excavations which have begun with this laudable aim have run out of time or money or both before the bottom has been reached, and the earliest occupation levels have had to be abandoned. It is tempting to linger on the detail of well-preserved eighteenth-century house plans or to dig large medieval rubbish pits, thin layer by thin layer, but when there is only one month left and hitherto unsuspected prehistoric buildings begin to emerge, one has second thoughts about the importance of medieval rubbish, especially if the pits have been virtually empty of finds.

Those who plan excavations have, therefore, very difficult choices to make. For the sake of those who are financing them, excavations must be as cost effective as possible, which means getting as much reliable evidence per pound sterling as possible. The work-force, also, must be employed as effectively as possible if their time is not be wasted; excavation is hard, exacting work for trowellers, recorders, draughtsmen, finds assistants, photographers and everyone else, and their talents and skills must not be dissipated on work which is hardly worth doing.

The importance of pre-excavation methods of assessing the site's potential will be obvious. Unfortunately, even if all the methods at present available are deployed, they can only provide a rough guide to the complexity of the archaeological layers which may be encountered. Clearly, a site with three metres of stratified deposits is likely to take a good deal longer to dig than one with only a few centimetres. However, some sites have many periods of occupation stratified within a large number of very thin layers, each one of which has to be dealt with separately if the sequence is to be understood. Apart from the actual mass of soil to be removed, which must, of course, be taken into account, it is the *number* of layers and features which determines how long it will take to dig the site, rather than simply the depth of the stratification. The bailey of the timber castle at Hen Domen, Montgomery, has taken a very long while to dig, simply because the layers are thin, and the uppermost, that is the latest, occupation levels have been defined by spreads of pebbles and other slight features, all of which have had to be meticulously cleaned and recorded (see Figs. 36a and, from Wroxeter, 79a). Even sites which in trial sections look fairly straightforward often prove to be very much more complicated when they are dug, and crop-mark sites are always immensely more so (see Figs. 25 and 26).

Excavation strategy must be based, first of all, on the best available knowledge of the site before it is dug, when a series of questions can be formulated. These questions – such as 'What is the length of occupation on the site?', 'What is the nature of the occupation?', 'Is there continuity of occupation between the earliest and latest phases?' – and so on, which are generally applicable to almost every site, can be followed by more specific questions to be asked of the site under consideration. These will, of course, depend on the nature of the site. In a town, one might ask if the Roman defences pass through the site, or if the site is within or outside the limits of the Roman defences. Or one might ask if the town can be shown to have had a prehistoric forerunner, or if the church known to have been in the vicinity is there or elsewhere, or what evidence there is for the changing economy of the town, and so on. On a rural site, the questions may be more specifically economic or be concerned with the evidence of climatic change with the growth and desertion of, for example, a medieval village. Yet whatever questions may be asked before excavation begins, the excavator must be prepared to add to them or change them as the excavation develops. The deserted medieval village may begin to produce unequivocal evidence of Roman occupation underlying the medieval house sites. Inevitably, then, the question which poses itself will be 'What is the relationship between the

Roman occupation and the medieval village?', and, following that, 'Is there continuity of settlement through the thousand years that separate them, or is it merely coincidental?', 'What is the nature of the field systems of the two settlements, their boundaries and the sizes of their fields?', 'Can any major differences in their economies be detected?' and 'If there are differences, why?', and so on.

In other cases the questions which might be asked will dictate which, out of a number of sites, shall be excavated and which left either undug, or with only a watching brief as they are destroyed (see Chapter 5). This might be the case, for instance, in a town where the existence of a Saxon *burh* is known from the documentary evidence. Worcester is a case in point, a *burh* having been unequivocally established in the latter part of the ninth century. Although the area of the *burh* can be estimated and its general position in relation to the later medieval city can be assumed, nothing is known of the precise line of the defences, or of their nature, nor anything about the buildings within the *burh*. Under these circumstances, if two sites become available for excavation, and one promises to lie across the line of the *burh* defences, with an area inside them as well, these may be the deciding factors in choosing this, rather than the other site. Of course, it is likely that in a city such as Worcester, with a history stretching back into prehistoric times, any site within the medieval walls will have strong claims to be dug, and the decision to choose one site rather than another will be made correspondingly harder.

It will be appreciated, then, that the devising of a national research strategy based on rescue priorities is even more difficult, as the problems are all compounded. Nevertheless, this must be the ultimate aim, if our diminishing archaeological resource – our sites and ancient landscapes – is to be properly managed.

CHAPTER THREE

Pre-excavation research

NON-DESTRUCTIVE SITE EXAMINATION

Until comparatively recently, digging on site began with the minimum of pre-excavation research. If earthworks were being dug, the obvious targets were entrances with a section or two across the ramparts of defended sites. Crop-mark sites were dug at selected points where the crop-marks were clearest, or looked most interesting. Often, the reasons for digging a particular site were non-archaeological – the fact that the site belonged to the excavator or his neighbour, or that it was the local land-mark or a newly-discovered crop-mark of special interest to the excavator. There was little sense of an overall national or even regional strategy of research, though individuals from Pitt-Rivers to Wheeler had their own strategic projects. Now the situation is changing, partly because of the increased realization of the fact that each site is unique, and partly because the speed of destruction of sites and whole landscapes means that there are less sites every day, that we are dealing with a rapidly wasting asset, and that those sites which are dug, whether for 'rescue' or 'research', must therefore be dug with adequate pre-excavation preparation.

The more that non-destructive examination of sites can be developed, the more effective will be the subsequent excavation, and the better the use of money and resources, particularly of skilled people – the most valuable resource we have. The principal ways of examining monuments by non-destructive methods are outlined below.

1 *The study of relevant documents*
Documentary references to archaeological sites may simply be a passing reference to a prehistoric monument in an early manuscript, such as John Leland's 1542 reference to the hill-fort at South Cadbury, which he called Camallate (Camelot) (quoted in full in Alcock, 1975, p.11), or William Stukeley's drawing of the same site in 1723 (*ibid*. Plate 2). A

useful piece of evidence from Leland's description is that 'Much gold, sylver and coper of the Roman coynes hath been found ther in plouing . . .', suggesting at least Roman, if not later, occupation in an Iron Age fort; and Stukeley's drawing shows that, in his day, the ramparts were free of trees and undergrowth. His profile of the defences is more elaborate than at present and it may simply be that he did not count the ramparts correctly, but he was a good observer and it is worth considering that the lowest rampart that he shows has been lost to ploughing on the lower slopes.

At the other extreme, references to sites in towns may be very full, enabling an almost complete record to be built up of landlords and tenants, with their occupations. In this case, excavation may flesh out the documentary story by revealing the form and development of the successive buildings on the site and in so doing use the documents to help in their interpretation. In the choice of sites to be dug in a town, the site with the most complete documentation would always be given preference if all other factors were equal.

Castles are often very well documented, but sometimes for only one or two periods of their occupation. The earliest buildings have often been replaced long ago, and their excavation not only extends the history of the site backwards, but puts them into its context by reference to the documentary description. Here again, given a number of similar sites, it is those with firm documentation which will take precedence; even one documentary mention may be of crucial importance in the choice of site. The motte and baily castle now called Hen Domen, Montgomery, was chosen for excavation because of two entries in the Domesday Book for Shropshire, which mention it by name, one saying that 'the earl [Roger de Montgomery] himself has here constructed a castle, which he calls Montgomery' (after his birthplace in Normandy). Roger was made Earl of Shrewsbury in 1070 or 71, so the castle must have been built between then and 1086, the date of the Domesday Book. Since almost no other motte and bailey castles on the Welsh border are referred to in contemporary documents, the opportunity to excavate a castle whose date of building was very soon after the Conquest and is known to within 15 years, coupled with the fact that it was built by one of William the Conqueror's chief lieutenants, made it the obvious choice for long-term excavation (see Barker and Higham, 1982, esp. Chap. 3). There were, however, problems. We had taken it for granted, as had everyone before us, that Hen Domen was the first Montgomery Castle, but this view was challenged by a local archaeologist, and we had to do a good deal of further research before being able (we believe) to prove that they were one and the same (*ibid.*). So it is very important to be sure that the documentary references actually refer to the site that is about to be dug and not to a quite different one down the road.

2 *The study of old maps and drawings*
All archaeological sites are part of the landscape which surrounds them, and the best excavators study the site's context as well as the site itself. An invaluable source of information about the landscape of the last two centuries can be found in Estate Maps and Terriers, in the Tithe Maps with their Apportionment (which gives the names of fields and their owners), and in the early editions of the Ordnance Survey. From these and from field-work in the neighbourhood, a picture of the landscape of which the site is a part can be built up. This is important, since no site is isolated from the fields, woods or hamlets which surround it, and on which, in varying degrees, it depends.

The maps may have crucial information about the site itself, showing changes which have occurred since the map was drawn or showing that features which were thought to have been modern are at least as old as the map.

Sometimes engravings or watercolour drawings of the site exist in local, or even national, collections. The views of castles made by the brothers Buck in the eighteenth century are well-known sources of information about the state of the castles then, and churches and abbeys were favourite subjects for artists. Here again, however, there are pitfalls. Dr Warwick Rodwell has drawn attention to two illustrations of the tower of the church of St Peter, Barton-on-Humber, where one illustration, made partly to prove the author's theories, can be shown to have a number of fundamental inaccuracies when compared with the other (he has not even managed to count the arches in a blind arcade correctly . . . (Rodwell, 1981, fig. 8, p. 22).

The seventeenth-century town maps of Speed and Roque are invaluable sources of information, particularly about street patterns, but often giving details of buildings now lost, or the line of town defences. In most towns there are maps of many dates, scattered through the last three centuries, and from them can be built up a picture of the town's development, or, from the point of view of an excavation, the development of a street frontage or tenement, to be supplemented by the excavation, which will, hopefully, take the story back beyond the days when maps were made.

3 *Previous work on site*
Many archaeological sites have been dug into in the past two centuries. Only too often there is no record of the excavation, and this has to be found when digging begins, but in other cases there may be a report in the local Archaeological Society's *Transactions*, or the local paper, or in the local history collections of the relevant library or record office. Unfortunately, few early excavators, professional or amateur, left plans of the exact positions of their trenches, and their interpretations of their excavations often prove to be wildly inaccurate. Nevertheless, much can be gleaned from even the most inadequate report, especially if it is

accompanied by measured drawings. Positive evidence – the inclusion of
a layer, or a wall, or a pit – is more to be trusted than an omission, which
may have happened because the excavator did not notice or understand
the evidence. All the previous trenches dug on the site of the Baths
Basilica at Wroxeter, currently being dug by the writer (August, 1985),
have had to be found by trowelling, yet the reports of these early
excavations, from Thomas Wright to Kathleen Kenyon, have been
informative when used with care, and their trenches, when emptied in
advance of the present excavation, have given very valuable information
about what is to come.

4 *Aerial photographs*
Archaeological aerial photography has made some of the most
spectacular advances of the past half century in our knowledge of the
number and variety of archaeological sites here in Britain and abroad.
Hundreds of sites have been dug *because* their potential was discovered
from aerial photographs, and, in many other cases, aerial photography
has helped to decide where, on a large site, digging would be most
productive. Aerial photographs often indicate the potential of a site, but
almost always sites prove to be far more complex and difficult than they
look from the air, so that aerial photography only shows the *minimal*
potential of a site; its real potential is almost always much greater (see
Collfryn in Fig.25; Beckford in Fig.26, and Wroxeter in Fig.30).

5 *Field walking*
If the site has recently been ploughed, it is worthwhile walking the field
systematically to pick up pottery and other finds. In some cases a thick
scatter of roof tile in one part of the field may be a clear indication of a
collapsed building. In many cases, however, the evidence will be a little
more elusive – an increase in the scatter of pot-sherds or flints will be the
only evidence for occupation. It is necessary to devise a method of
collection which can be recorded in areas sufficiently precise to be
registered on a map of the field, so that the density of all finds can be
assessed. For those interested, discussion of field-walking methods will
be found in Fasham, 1980 and DoE Occasional Paper 2, 1980. It is
interesting to note that in a systematic survey of part of the valley of the
Warwickshire Avon consisting of a large group of fields, many of which
contained a mass of crop-marks, all the fields were walked and, in more
than one instance, it was the fields without crop-marks which yielded the
most pottery, so that the methods proved to be complementary, and
showed that virtually the whole valley was full of early occupation.
Nevertheless, both photographs and pot scatters showed varying
densities, on which decisions as to where to excavate could have been
made.

[67

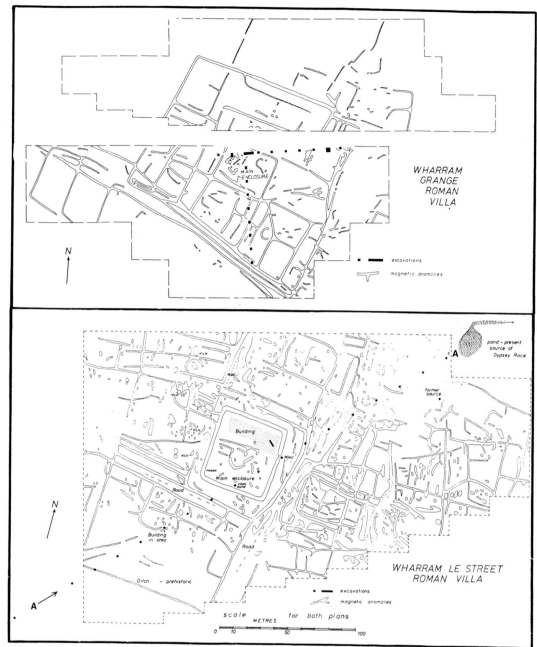

WHARRAM
GRANGE
ROMAN
VILLA

N

excavations
magnetic anomalies

pond ~ present
source of
Gypsey Race

former
source

KILN

ROAD

KILN

KILN

Building

KILN

ROAD

mosaic

Main enclosure

Road

N

Building
in area

Road

A

Road

Ditch ~ prehistoric

WHARRAM LE STREET
ROMAN VILLA

A

excavations
magnetic anomalies

scale for both plans
METRES
0 10   50   100

Fig. 28

Fig. 28 *Wharram Roman villas*
These are on the chalk wolds in
Eastern Yorkshire, 2 kilometres each
side of the well-known medieval
village site of Wharram Percy. Each
villa was explored by four techniques:
aerial photography, geophysical
surveying, fieldwalking of the
ploughed soil, and excavation. The
first three provided in each case an
excellent framework, showing the
broad outline plan of the site, and a
spread of Roman pottery and building
materials. Excavation elucidated this

general picture, providing useful data
on pre-Roman activity (back to the
mesolithic); the depth and character of
archaeological stratification; the
nature and depth of the subsoil; the
range of building material used in the
villas; many coins and other finds to
show the standard of living and date
range of the occupation; and details of
infant burial, tesselated floors, ditches
and roads.
The method used was to dig rows of
1 metre square boxes, and record these
meticulously (A-A on Fig. 28).

The excavation was of only 25 square
metres on each site, was done in four
days with about ten people on each
site, and cost about £400. Together
with the other three methods of
investigation, they provided a very
useful sample of the history of each
site, assisting materially in current
planning and protection schemes, and
providing a useful picture for later
more extensive excavations.
The work of these two digs has
resulted in a publication of
monograph size!

Fig. 29a

Figs. 29a,b,c and **d**   These illustrate the examination of a small field, C, next to the motte and bailey castle at Hen Domen, Montgomery. Excavations under the rampart of the castle bailey at B had shown that the ridge and furrow cultivation of the northern field, A, continued under the rampart, proving that the ploughing was pre-Norman in date. Further evidence suggests that it was probably of the tenth century. This, and other aerial photographs, taken in glancing light (at 2.30 pm on Boxing Day, 1984, to be precise), showed that field C also was full of ridge and furrow. However, this ridging was not nearly so obvious from the ground – what appeared more clearly was a group of three small platforms at D (in the photograph

unfortunately in the long shadows of the tree on the other side of the road). It was first considered that these platforms might be the site of the small settlement whose inhabitants ploughed the pre-Conquest fields. However, the aerial photograph shows clearly that the ridging runs right across the platforms, so that these must be earlier. They may, nevertheless, belong to a settlement relating to an earlier form of the field system.

A contour survey of field C was made in 1973 and plotted (by Susan Laflin) with the aid of the main-frame computer at the University of Birmingham, and the results are shown graphically in a three-dimensional display from each of the

field's four sides in turn (**Fig. 29c**). (The contours are at 10cm vertical intervals above the temporary bench mark.) These plots show the ridging, but not so clearly as on the aerial photograph. One of them, but only one (number 2), shows the small platforms at D. Yet these were more obvious to the eye than the ridging.

In 1972 a fluxgate magnetometer survey was carried out to try to detect magnetic anomalies, such as hearths, pits or ditches. The results are shown in **Fig. 29d**, and it can be seen that they bear no relation to the visible earthworks, except that the apparent ditch, G, runs roughly parallel to the outer ditch and counterscarp rampart of the motte, F. It is possible, therefore, that it is a previously undetected marking-out ditch dug to indicate the line of the defences to the ditch-diggers. It may, on the other hand, be a slot in which an outer palisade stood. The other anomalies, at H, I, J, and K, do not seem to have any obvious connection with the castle and may be connected with the slight hollows close to them; or they may, of course, be part of another, altogether different, phase of occupation here. In fact, the hollow-way, L-L, which at its southern end rises up on to a small causeway, seems to be sited deliberately between the two obliterated ditches, I and J. Whether this is simply coincidental can be solved only by excavation. It is perhaps also significant that the 'pits' grouped together at K are all south of ditch J, which suggests that they are outside (or perhaps inside) whatever is bounded by ditches I and J. The small ditch-like anomly at H cannot be explained without excavation.

The lesson which we have learned from this quite intensive study of what is really a very small field is that no one method of investigation tells all – the field was photographed from the air for many years before the slight ridging showed up; studying the surface from the ground and from the air gave no hint of the ditches and pits revealed by the magnetic survey. And there is no doubt at all that excavation would, in an attempt to solve these problems, reveal new ones. A further complication is that excavation here would be inhibited by the fact that this is one of the very few areas of provable pre-Norman ridge and furrow in Britain, so that there is every reason to leave these problems permanently unsolved, since the proper excavation of the field would destroy its chief asset. It would, of course, be possible to pin-point the ditches and pits and excavate them in isolation, but, though this might produce some finds and some dating evidence, it would not be likely to tell us anything about the circumstances in which they were dug, or to what nearby occupation they related. All experience shows that

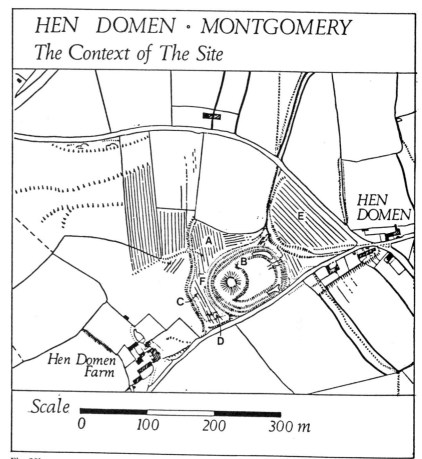

Fig. 29b

the evidence produced by the magnetometer survey (like that produced by aerial photography) is likely to be only the tip of the iceberg. (Photo: C.R. Musson)

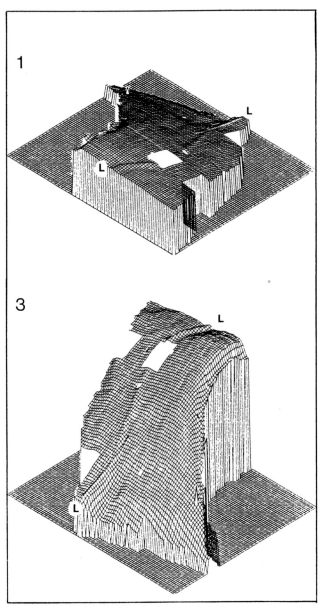
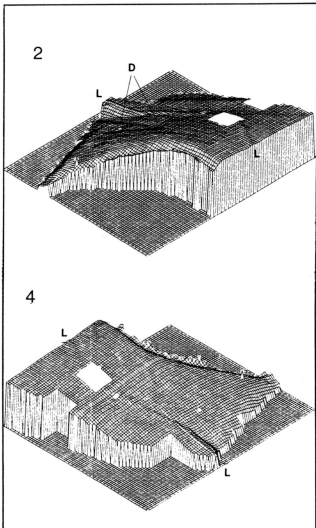

Fig. 29c

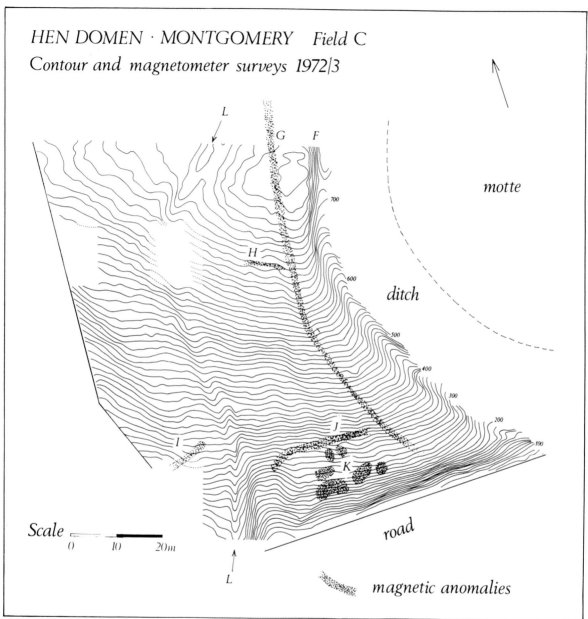

HEN DOMEN · MONTGOMERY   Field C
Contour and magnetometer surveys 1972/3

Scale

0   10   20m

magnetic anomalies

Fig. 29d

Figs. 30a,b and **c,** In the mid-second century the city of Wroxeter was almost doubled in size with a new defensive line, a-a, being drawn north of the Bell Brook. The very large area thus added does not seem to have included any metalled streets or stone buildings north of the valley in which the little Bell Brook runs. However, a series of very fine aerial photographs by Arnold Baker, of which **Figs. 30a** and **b** are two, shows what appears to be a grid of ditches or gullies within the defences, together with a multiplicity of pits of all sizes, many of them rectilinear (and therefore not, for example, tree root holes). There appears to have been intensive occupation here, but in timber buildings rather than stone. However, the immediate impression of a grid of streets has a misleading element, since it is overlain by ridge and furrow (which can be seen clearly outside the defences). Nevertheless, when the ridge and furrow has, as it were, been subtracted from the total picture, the pattern of pits, ditches and gullies which is left is still rectilinear and argues for a planned extension of the city into this northern sector.

Outside the defences, converging trackways, enclosures, and, in particular, enclosed cemeteries b, b can be seen. What is remarkable is that the outer pattern of crop-marks bears no relation to that inside and, since the spread of the counterscarp rampart obliterates the outer crop-marks, these must be earlier. The trackways disappear under the defences at c and do not reappear inside (there is no trace of a gate), so it is clear that the enlargement of the city not only erased the earlier landscape but denied access at this point to the cemeteries. These must, therefore, themselves be early and perhaps even disused and forgotten by the time of the enlargements. It is apparent also that the trackways cut across some of the enclosure crop-marks which may, of course, be pre-Roman.

The intensively occupied area shown in Fig. 30c covers some 360,000 square

Fig. 30a

metres or 36 hectares – nearly 90 acres. It is very probable that, as in all crop-mark sites (see Collfryn, Fig. 25 and Beckford Fig. 26), the complexity of the evidence and the depth of stratification would prove to be many times greater than appears on the photograph. The current excavation of the Baths Basilica site in the city centre (Figs. 43 and 83) covers some 5,600sq m or a little over half a hectare – about 1⅓ acres – and it has taken some 19 seasons' work with an average labour force of 90 people working for five weeks each year (8550 worker-weeks) to excavate the upper levels only, those layers which represent the period from *c.* AD 300 to *c.* AD 500. On the assumption that it would take as long again to reach the beginnings of the city's occupation, it would then

take 17,000 worker-weeks to excavate the whole site. Simple arithmetic suggests that it would take in the order of 1,224,000 worker-weeks to excavate the area shown in the photograph. Even if this estimate is wrong by a factor of ten, it is clear that the excavation of even this part of the city, about a third of the total, would be an immense task. The defences alone have proved, in recent excavations, to need digging on a scale commensurate with their size, if they are not simply to pose more questions than they solve. There has been an understandable tendency in the past to concentrate on Roman city centres, their baths and fora, their shops, theatres and amphitheatres (if they had them). But a complete picture of town life in Roman Britain should include the

Fig. 30b

suburbs, the cemeteries, and the surrounding farms which provided much of the city's food and the raw materials for its workshops, since a city such as Wroxeter comprises a vast range of trades and industries, as well as commerce from most parts of the Empire, even from as far away as the eastern Mediterranean.

Large sample excavations, perhaps amounting to a total of a quarter of the whole, might be sufficient to establish the nature of the occupation within the outside of the defences, and solve outstanding problems of the defences themselves. But the cemeteries would have to be completely excavated if they were to provide a full and unequivocal picture of their occupants. Smaller, carefully devised sampling strategies would provide viable environmental evidence in the form of seeds, pollen, insects, snails and so on over a larger range than the area excavations. The question which must be asked is whether all this very considerable expenditure of labour and money would be worthwhile? There is no doubt that such a programme, allied to similar

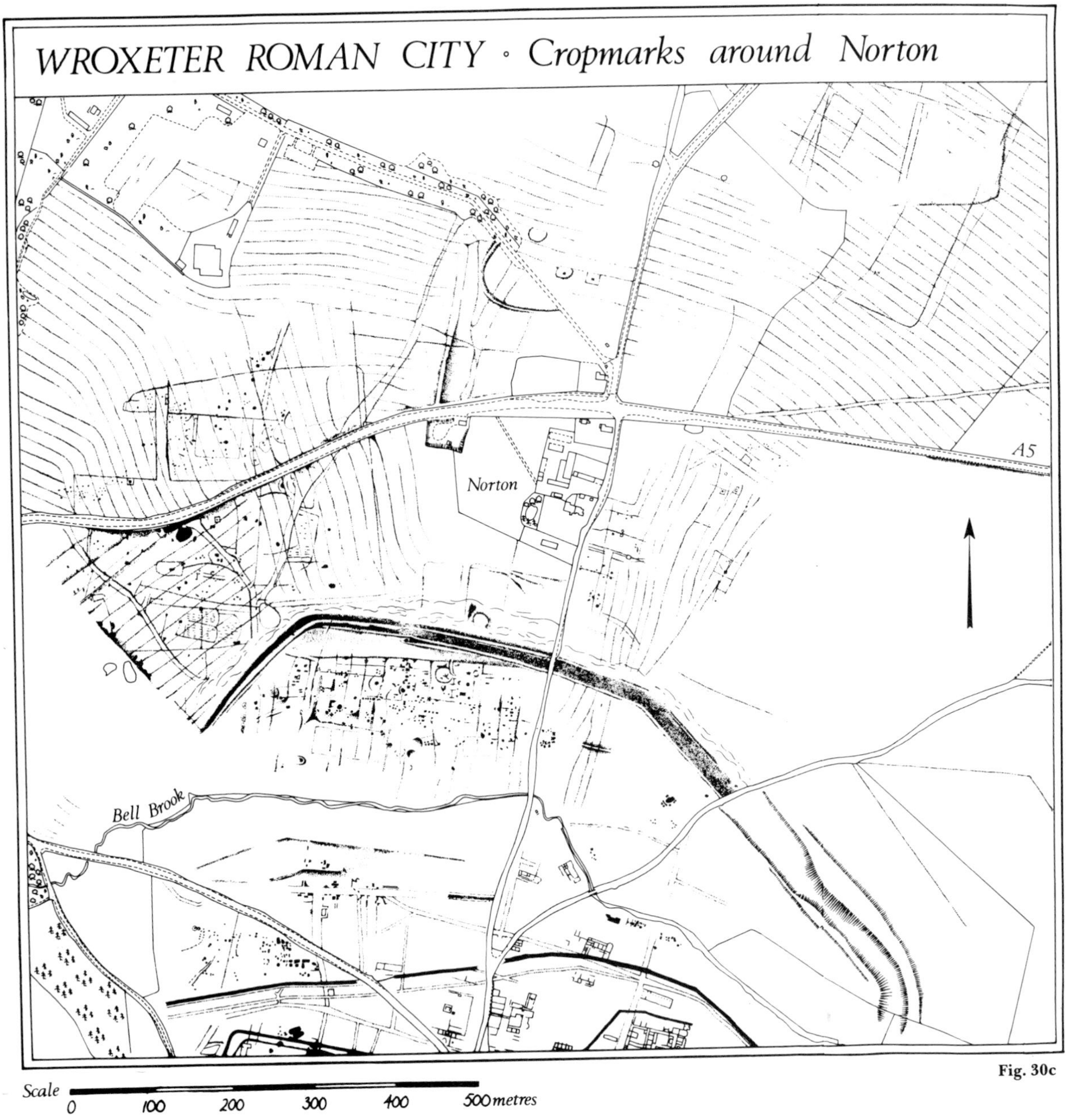

WROXETER ROMAN CITY · Cropmarks around Norton

Norton

A5

Bell Brook

Scale
0   100   200   300   400   500 metres

Fig. 30c

excavations in the rest of the city, would provide a vivid and highly detailed picture of life in Roman Britain. If this were displayed to the public in simple graphic terms using all the resources of modern technology, the result could be dramatic. The same could be said of many other sites – deserted medieval villages such as Wharram Percy (Fig. 37a), great hillforts such as Maiden Castle, or British Camp, Malvern, (Fig. 17).

6 *Contour surveying*

A close contour survey of the site to be excavated is a necessity for a number of reasons. First, it is the best way to present an accurate plan of the site in the eventual report; second, it may well reveal features of the site which might otherwise be missed; and third, if the site has to be reinstated when the excavation is finished, it provides the best record on which the reinstatement can be based. It also provides data for the building of a model for museum display (see Fig. 25f).

7 *Geophysical methods of site survey*

These are methods which detect underground anomalies, such as wells, pits, gullies, ditches, walls, floors, hearths, kilns and roads. Resistivity meters measure the differences in electrical resistivity between terminals driven into the ground at intervals – pits, ditches and gullies, which are normally filled with damp humic soil, offer less resistance to the current than walls, roads and floors. If the readings are taken on a grid covering the whole site, the varying resistances can be plotted as a series of contours, or simply as anomalies or features. Similarly, the same anomalies or features tend to carry a detectably different magnetic field from that of the earth's magnetic field. Hearths and kilns (or burnt down buildings), in particular, have a strong local magnetic effect, though pits, ditches and roads etc. can also be detected. The magnetic anomalies can be plotted in a number of ways to reveal their pattern. An example is illustrated in Fig.29d. In a similar way, radar and sonar are being used to add to these non-destructive methods of site exploration. Of particular interest is a soil-sounding radar, developed by Mike Gorman at Cambridge, which is being used at Sutton Hoo, where all the available methods of non-destructive sensing are being used on a site which is sensitive not only to all these methods but also to public opinion regarding its excavation (see Brothwell and Higgs, 1969).

8 *Phosphate and other chemical analyses*

Animal excreta and other organic remains contain quantities of detectable phosphates, and there have been a number of experiments in sampling the quantities of phosphates in the soil of suspected occupation sites in the hope of showing the intensity of occupation or isolating those areas occupied by animals, either in pens or in the byre ends of long-houses (see Gurney, 1986). There have been some successes with chemical detection methods, though they are by no means uniform, and will, of course, be dependent to a great extent on the subsoil and the climate, since there is much more leaching of chemicals through the soil in, say, a wet climate on a sandy subsoil than in a dry climate on rock. Another experiment which has been tried with mixed success is to attempt to detect oak beams which have simply lain on the ground as foundations, by testing for traces of tannin in the soil. There is no doubt that chemical methods of detection are in their infancy, and that the next few decades are likely to see rapid advances in this field.

9 *Metal detectors*

Metal detectors (or, more particularly, those who use them to rob sites of their metal objects) have rightly been condemned by archaeologists and others interested in recovering the whole picture of a site, and not just its more desirable (and saleable) objects. Metal detectors are, however, akin to magnetometers and can be used in conjunction with them. At Sutton Hoo, they are used to screen out stray metal objects, leaving the larger anomalies found by the magnetometers, while radar resolves the deep and shallow anomalies (Carver, 1984).

Some archaeologists have set their faces firmly against those who use metal detectors; others have attempted to join with them, to explain what archaeology really is, and to enlist their help. Unfortunately, there is a hard core of professional treasure-hunters who loot sites systematically. These, not surprisingly, give all metal-detecting a bad name, and make it harder for those who wish to help in site prospection to be accepted.

10 *Dowsing*

Dowsing with hazel twigs or copper rods has been used from time immemorial to find water, wells, pipes and drains, and it certainly works. Whether it is a sound basis on which to plan an excavation is another matter. The writer has no experience of an excavation with a successful strategy based on dowsing; however, three of us, working independently with copper rods, found the same east-facing apsidal shape in the nave of Worcester Cathedral. This was promising because somewhere under the cathedral are two Anglo-Saxon minsters, no traces of which have ever been seen. Unfortunately, when we came to dig where the apsidal structure should have been, there was nothing resembling it. One of our number, having more faith in the rods than the rest, said that the apse had been dug away in antiquity and that we had traced the place where it had been, its 'ghost' . . .

BORE HOLES

Many contractors bore test holes in sites before development in order to examine the underlying strata, since they need to know as much as possible before designing buildings, especially multi-storey ones. Archaeologists can often use these borings to obtain a preview of the nature and depth of the occupation layers and the nature of the undisturbed subsoil. There may be snags, however – one bore hole in the centre of Worcester went through 32ft (9.7m) of black earth (it had probably gone straight down a well . . .). And during the examination of the foundations of the central tower of Worcester Cathedral excavations had shown that the piers were founded on massive blocks of beautifully built masonry surrounded by packed gravel (Fig. 14). But a bore hole drilled exactly in the centre part between the tower piers found nothing like this – simply layers of rubble and then the subsoil. From this it is clear that the builders of the tower dug not one but four enormous holes, constructed the masonry foundations and packed them with gravel, before building the tower, thus:

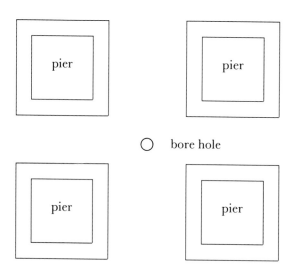

pier

pier

○ bore hole

pier

pier

Boreholes can, then, be very informative but suffer from the same limitations as trenches and test-pits – it is dangerous to extrapolate far beyond the point which is tested.

TRIAL TRENCHES AND TEST-PITS

Trial trenches have for decades been the standard method of sampling a site; of seeing whether it was what it appeared to be; of testing the depth of the stratification; of obtaining a sample of the pottery and finds so as to be able to decide whether or not to continue with a larger excavation.

Trenches and pits have many limitations – one is illustrated in Figs. 36b and c – but at the same time they do provide much information very quickly. In advance of a rescue excavation where time is limited a machine-dug trench may be necessary to prove, not only to the archaeologist himself, but to a Town Council, a landowner or even the Inspectorate of Ancient Monuments, that there really is something there that should either be dug before destruction or preserved for ever.

Inevitably, machine-dug trenches or pits destroy almost everything within the trench and the excavator has to rely chiefly on looking at the two sides of the trench or the four sides of the pit. Because pits have *four* sides some excavators prefer to dig a series of pits in line, a sort of discontinuous trench. In this way less damage is done to the site in the event of a full-scale excavation being carried out later . If time permits, trenches and pits can be dug slowly and by hand, in which case far more evidence can be recorded (see the examples from Wharram, Fig. 28 above). Hopefully, therefore, in the event of a larger excavation which encompasses the test holes, these can be incorporated in the stratigraphic record.

The siting of trial trenches and pits is also a matter for considerable thought. They can be taken deliberately across the major features of the site in order to sample them, though if these are, for example, the sort of buildings which it might be desirable to display later, it might be better to avoid the buildings and rely on sufficient evidence on which to make judgements being obtained from the spaces between. It would, after all, cause some red faces if, when sampling a Roman villa, the head of Christ in mosaic came up in the bull-dozer bucket. One major problem is that it is difficult to predict the spaces – what seems to be a space often contains a mass of features. The 'hollow-way' at Wharram shown in Fig. 37a might have been thought to be a fairly straightforward sunken road with few complications; Fig. 37b shows how mistaken this assumption would have been.

Sometimes it is possible to obtain a preview of the site without destroying it. For example, in a town there may well be cellars under demolished eighteenth-century or Victorian buildings. These cellars can be emptied of their rubble filling, and the walls removed, when four sections through the site, each 6ft (1.8m) or more deep, can be seen without any more damage than had been caused a century before.

In the same way, if it is known that disused sewers or drains or other services cross the site, the trenches in which they lie can be emptied, providing two long sections.

The problem with all trial trenches and pits is that they not only destroy areas of the site without them being understood but they also cut the stratification, divorcing one part of the site from another. If these cuts exist on the site already, in the form of old trenches or cellars or pits, the damage has been done and the maximum information should be gleaned from them without any further losses of evidence.

CHAPTER FOUR

Methods of excavation

The ideal excavation would extract from the site everything that could possibly be known about it – everything that has survived the physical and chemical changes of centuries of burial. So little is now left of the original house or village, cemetery or fort, that the methods of excavation used have to be increasingly refined – crude digging will only recover a tiny percentage of what is already reduced to a fraction. Only too often, excavations are hurried or partial, or carried out with a JCB instead of a teaspoon, because of factors which are quite outside the control of the archaeologist – an imminent development, a chance discovery or simply lack of resources.

There is an unresolvable conflict between proper excavation and the need for speed, since there is an optimum speed at which the excavation can be carried out – the site, of whatever sort, should dictate the speed of the excavation. To try to go two or three times as fast without serious loss is like asking a surgeon to carry out a heart operation in half an hour with a knife and fork. This is because archaeological sites are immensely complicated, and those that appear simple have usually been made so by inadequate excavation.

On the other hand, the total excavation and recording of every facet of the site, from the documentation of the size, shape, weight and geology of every pebble to the recovery of every seed and every grain of pollen, is clearly unnecessary, even ludicrous, and certainly not cost-effective in either cash or the time of skilled personnel. So a balance has to be struck between the sweeping butchery of many earlier excavations and the necessary recovery of a minimum of highly detailed information. To strike this balance is the role of the director and his team. It might, for example, be decided after discussion with the specialists concerned to recover every possible animal bone, but to sample the seeds and pollen, the snails and oyster shells. In earlier days pottery was 'sampled' by throwing away all but the rim and base sherds. This is now unacceptable, because of the considerable losses of information which result; but it is now realized that wet-sieving (see Fig. 67) produces a large number of sherds which have been missed even by experienced trowellers and by dry-sieving. Furthermore, experiments have shown that, understandably, far more red sherds, even tiny ones, are recovered with the trowel and in the dry-sieve than black or grey ones, and that far more sherds of all kinds are missed in wet weather than in dry, because of the thin film of mud that obscures them. It will be appreciated, therefore, that even in this small area of research, the ideal excavation is very difficult to achieve.

I believe, though not all my colleagues agree with me, that the larger the continuous area of excavation can be, the more complete and undistorted the results will be. For example, there is no doubt that, if we could have excavated the bailey of the small motte and bailey castle at Hen Domen, Montgomery, as a whole we should have understood it more easily, and not lost evidence along the balk between the two quadrants which we have already excavated (Barker and Higham 1982, p.23). All experience shows that wherever there is an edge or a balk there is some loss of evidence, either because of simple erosion or because of the great difficulty of matching the two parts together, even if they have been dug with great care and meticulously recorded. However, one problem is that few archaeological sites have natural edges. Even apparently self-contained monuments, such as burial mounds, motte and bailey castles or churches, extend, archaeologically, beyond their obvious limits, as many excavations have shown.

What for instance, are the limits of a Roman town? Not the defences – there are almost certainly suburbs beyond, and the defences themselves very probably overlie earlier occupation which spreads beyond them (see Fig. 30c, Wroxeter air photograph plot). Nor can a single *insula* or block within the town be considered an isolatable unit. You might think that an excavation which had edges down the middle of the streets dividing the *insulae* would be self-contained, but at Wroxeter we should never have understood the remarkable late development of the east-west street if the excavation had not included it complete – though in doing so, it sliced off the fronts of the buildings facing the street, so that a subsequent excavator may have great difficulty joining his excavation to ours along this edge.

On the other hand, some sites have edges because the surrounding area has been destroyed, or because it is not available, nor is ever likely to be. Such a case may be a site in a town, with the houses on both sides occupied and likely to remain so. The excavation has, therefore, to be confined within that area, though it is very likely that underlying Roman or prehistoric occupation will not respect those limits.

Because I believe that the larger the horizontal area which can be excavated, the more the evidence will be understood, so I believe that trenches will almost always give partial and probably misleading answers. Compare an excavation with the dissection of a human body.

[*89*

Figs. 31 shows a case of salvage excavation. It is of a massive hole dug in the middle of the city of Worcester in 1965 – part of the destruction of the city centre castigated in the press as the Rape of Worcester. Observation of the machine excavation, plus a little controlled digging, showed the existence here of a series of large defensive ditches dating from the Iron Age and Roman times. Part of the latest Roman ditch lies in the shadow, marked b. Although the archaeology was carried out under the worst possible conditions, it nevertheless established the defensive circuits of prehistoric and Roman Worcester over a long stretch and enabled the rest of the circuits to be confidently assumed.
(photo: author)

Fig. 31

Fig. 32 In spite of the increasing use of sophisticated hardware, the principal excavation tool is still the trowel – usually a small one with a 3-4in (7.5-10cm) blade. Sometimes much smaller implements, for example dental tools, together with brushes of all sizes down to tiny paint brushes, are used for very fine detail, such as the cleaning of a skeleton or a small find *in situ*.
(Photo: Sidney Renow)

Fig. 32

Fig. 33

Fig. 33 This is a good example of fine trowelling. The grooves are the remains of a series of wooden water pipes and conduits which ran down the side of one of the streets in the Roman city of Wroxeter. The wood has disappeared, leaving its outlines preserved in the sandy matrix in which it had been laid. Crude or insensitive trowelling would have destroyed this ephemeral evidence.
(Photo: Sidney Renow)

Figs. 34a, b and **c** These three photographs show the emptying of a rubble-filled hollow in the north aisle of the Baths Basilica at Wroxeter. This revealed the remains of the mosaic floor which had slumped, probably into an underlying, badly-filled rubbish pit. In places where the floor had sunk, the mosaics were preserved by the subsequent levelling-up. Elsewhere, they had disappeared long before the end of Roman times, and **34b** shows the state of the floor in the first half of the fourth century AD, whilst **34c** shows the largest mosaic after cleaning.
(Photos: author)

Fig. 34a

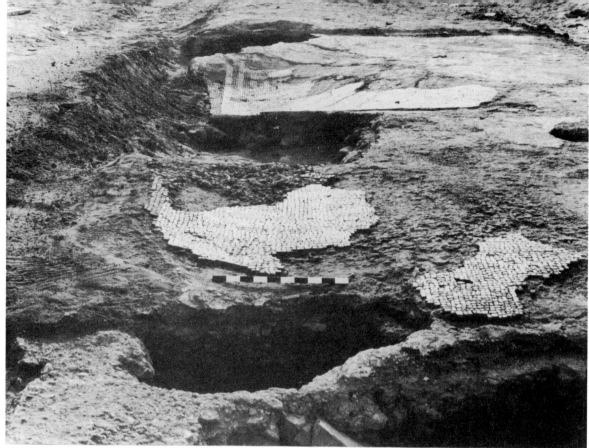

Fig. 34b

Fig. 34c

Fig. 35

Fig. 35 Plan of part of the excavation of a native village of Roman date at Wijster in Holland (van Es, 1967). The site was stripped mechanically, and then cleaned by labourers (as distinct from students or volunteers) using long-handled spades. The resulting mass of features was interpreted partly on the basis of patterns (for example, the large long-house in the centre of the figure), and partly on the incidence of overlapping features, on the basis of the argument that, if one feature cuts another, it must be later. In the upper part of the figure, at X, a sub-rectangular enclosure with rounded corners can be seen to cut some features, e.g. the fences which run northward, and to be cut by others, notably a large pit on its eastern side. So a chronological pattern, supplementing the structural pattern, is built up.

Figs. 36, 37 and **38**   *Trenching and gridding*
The easiest way to explain the uses and limitations of trenching and gridding is by a series of illustrations. **Fig. 36a** is a plan of an area of the bailey or courtyard of the timber castle at Hen Domen, Montgomery. About a quarter of the bailey was stripped of its topsoil and the visible features planned. These were then removed and the underlying layers were cleaned and planned. This was the surface shown in **Fig. 36a** (Phase Y). It consisted mostly of pebbles with a few post-settings which are shown in black. The whole surface is shown in the drawing in **Fig. 36a**. As can be seen, the concentrations of pebbles of various sizes are not random, but have clearly been laid purposefully. **Fig. 36d** shows the excavator's interpretation of this surface. Building IV was a polygonal tower sited on the bulbous end of the bailey rampart – it had burnt down and imprinted itself on the surface by reddening the clay of which the rampart was built. Building VIII was a small rectangular building behind the rampart, approached by a pebble path, while IX has been interpreted as a three-cell chapel, with a polygonal apsidal end, close to a double-post-hole palisade, V, which ran parallel to the motte ditch. The functions of the other, subsidiary, structures is less clear. It will be seen, though, that it would have been very difficult to make any sense at all out of the partial evidence provided by trenching or gridding. A full account of this interpretation will be found in Barker and Higham, 1982, pp. 41-48.
In the past, the trench has been the most popular and common way of exploring archaeological sites. In **36b** it is imagined that a trench 10ft (3m) wide has been laid out at right angles to the bailey rampart to explore the interior of the bailey. It will be seen that, although the patterns of pebbles and post-holes would suggest structures, there would be no hope of understanding them.
When the excavation at Hen Domen

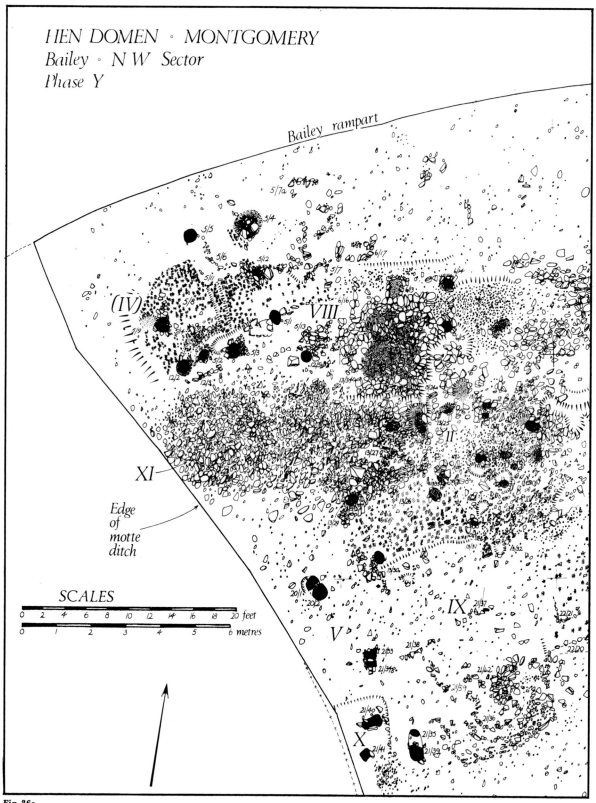

HEN DOMEN · MONTGOMERY
Bailey · N W Sector
Phase Y

Bailey rampart

(IV)

VIII

XI

Edge
of
motte
ditch

SCALES

0 2 4 6 8 10 12 14 16 18 20 feet
0   1   2   3   4   5   6 metres

II

IX

V

X

Fig. 36a

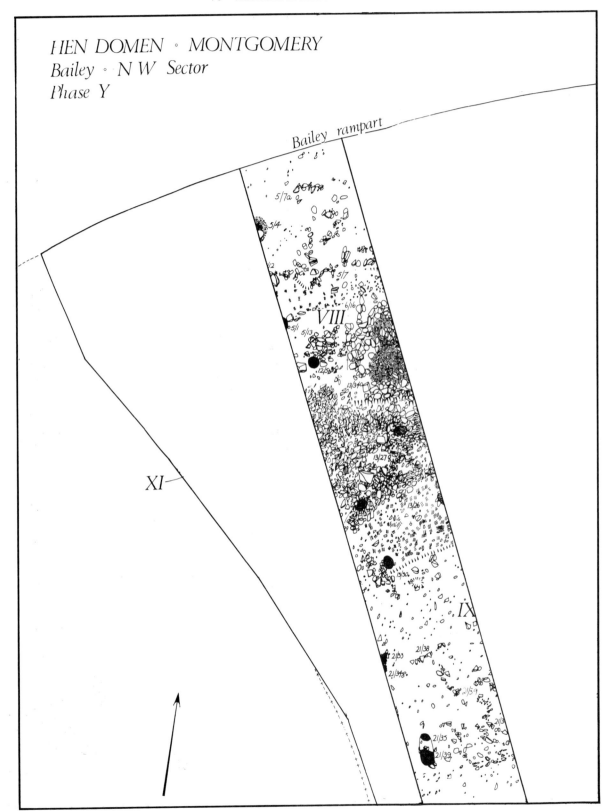

HEN DOMEN · MONTGOMERY
Bailey · N W Sector
Phase Y

Bailey rampart

5/7a

5/4

5/7

6/16

VIII

5/1   5/13

12/5

13/31

13/27

XI

13/26

13/32

IX

2/33   21/38

21/348

21/59

21/3

21/35

21/39

Fig. 36b

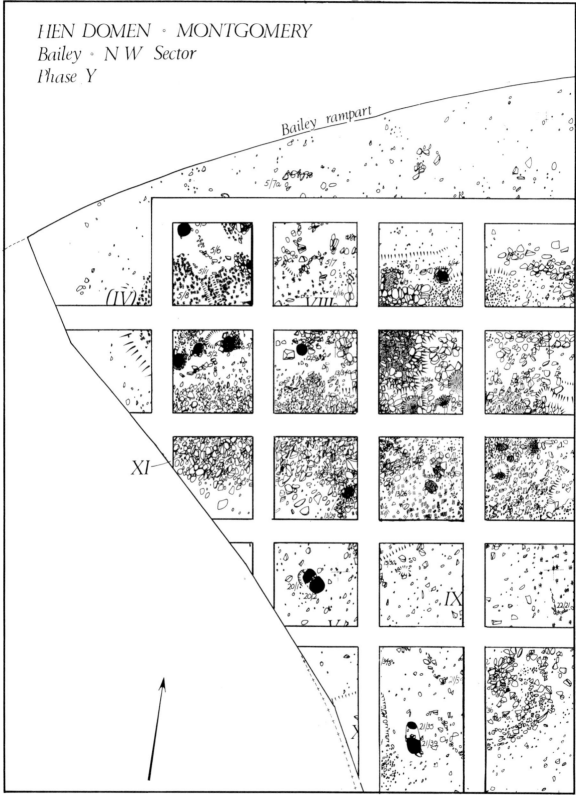

HEN DOMEN · MONTGOMERY
Bailey · N W Sector
Phase Y

Bailey rampart

Fig. 36c

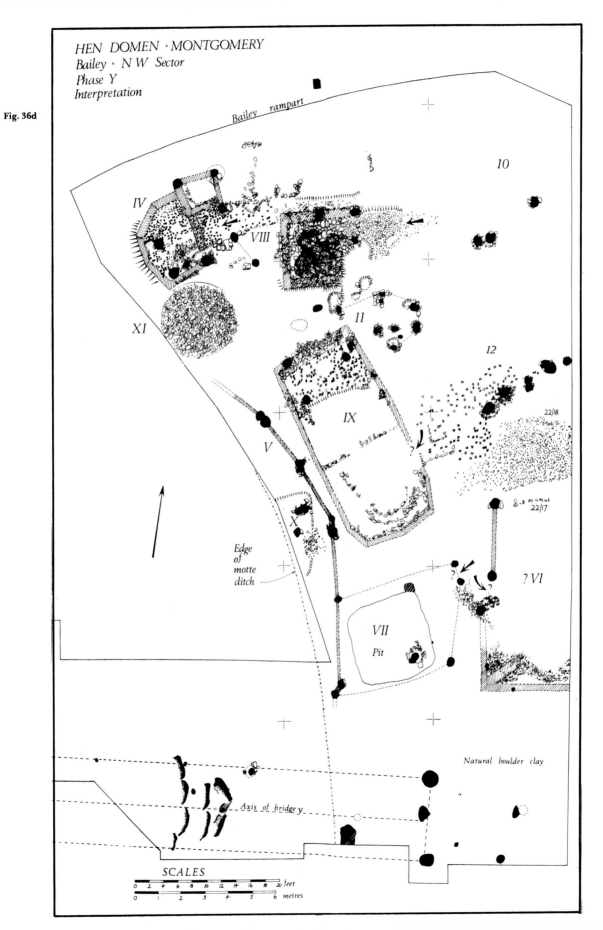

Fig. 36d

HEN DOMEN · MONTGOMERY
Bailey · N W Sector
Phase Y
Interpretation

Bailey rampart

IV

VIII

10

XI

11

12

IX

22/18

V

X

22/17

?VI

Edge
of
motte
ditch

VII
Pit

Natural boulder clay

Axis of bridge y

SCALES

0 2 4 6 8 10 12 14 16 18 20 feet

0   1   2   3   4   5   6 metres

began, the area was laid out in a series of grids, 10ft sq separated by balks 2ft wide. This was soon abandoned, as it was realized that it was producing distorted results (Barker and Higham, 1982, p. 23), but in **Fig. 36c** it is imagined that the grid system was continued into Phase Y. It will be seen immediately that it is virtually impossible to make sense of the features which are visible. In particular, Building IX could hardly be postulated from the evidence seen here. It would be clear that there was a series of structures of some sort – in particular the band of heavier stones running parallel to the rampart would be obvious, and the presence of buildings IV and VIII assumed, though their form would be impossible to describe.

The limitations of trenching and gridding on such a site are obvious, but the next example, **Figs. 37a** and **b** show how successful a wide trench, sited in the right place, can be. The medieval village of Wharram lies on the chalk Wolds of Eastern Yorkshire. The site is a large one, now under permanent Guardianship, and being developed for visitors to see the medieval village earthworks and ruined church and churchyard. It is the scene of one of the best-known excavations in Britain, which has been going on for over thirty years, for three weeks each year, with up to 100 people working at one time. Even with this massive input of research, time and labour, less than five per cent of the site has been dug. Certain areas have, however, been very rich in archaeological evidence. Between 1980 and 1984 in the North Manor area, a wide trench was cut by Philip Rahtz across a hollow-way, or sunken road (**Fig. 37a**). A sequence was recovered of: (a) a major defended late Iron Age settlement lying under the manor; (b) extensive Roman levels including a road and corn-dryer (there is probably a villa close by); (c) Early Saxon huts of the sixth century, cutting through the Roman road; (d) Late Saxon wooden buildings and

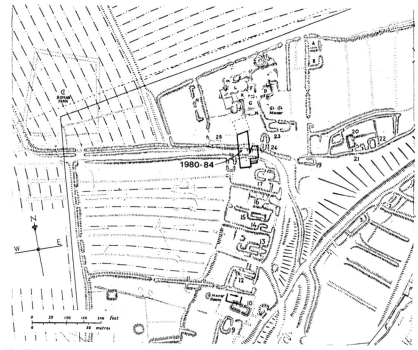

Fig. 37a

pottery, and (e) the medieval manor itself (**Fig. 37b**). The dig was only *c.* 400 square metres, a tiny fragment of Wharram, but a remarkable sample of its long history.

Another example of the uses of a single trench derives again from the work of Philip Rahtz (**Fig. 37c**). The castle at Kenilworth is one of the grandest of all castle ruins. Although its history was well known, and its architecture had been extensively studied, little was known about its archaeology below ground. The question to be solved by excavation was: what was the original ground level in the outer court? the 'answer' was much more complex. It would clearly, in this context, have been beyond the available resources to excavate the whole outer court, so a single trench, 5ft (1.60m) wide was cut across the court in 1960 (**Fig. 37d**). This revealed a remarkable sequence of two hitherto unsuspected major ditches, part of the twelfth- and thirteenth-century defences of the castle, buildings and occupation

levels, culminating in the massive destruction of the castle during the Parliamentary Civil War. It would, of course, be necessary to excavate horizontally, and much more extensively, in order to resolve the buildings and other occupation sequences, but the trench had made a major contribution to the understanding of the castle's defences. The dig was done by one archaeologist and four workmen in four weeks. The maximum depth was *c.* 5m, so the trench had to be extensively shored. It will be seen that such a trench is cost-effective in terms of the knowledge gained.

A linear earthwork excavated: **Fig. 38** is of the hollow-way, or sunken road, which runs up through the centre of a deserted village into the baileys of the castle at Stafford, seen on its motte in the background. During the course of the excavation of the village, the hollow-way was excavated in order to elucidate its construction and use. As will be seen, a narrow section across it

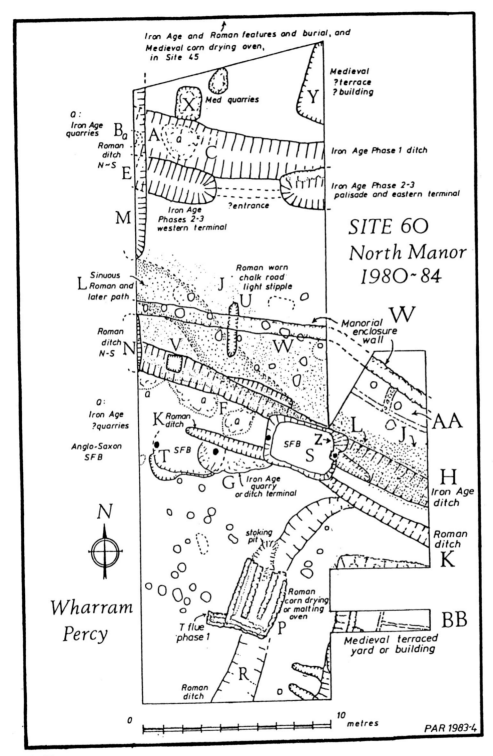

Iron Age and Roman features and burial, and
Medieval corn drying oven,
in Site 45

Medieval
?terrace
? building

Y

X Med quarries

Q:
Iron Age
quarries

B_a

A a

C

Roman
ditch
N~S

E

Iron Age Phase 1 ditch

Iron Age Phase 2-3
palisade and eastern terminal

M

Iron Age
Phases 2-3
western terminal

?entrance

SITE 60
North Manor
1980~84

Sinuous
Roman and
later path

L

Roman worn
chalk road
light stipple

J

U

Roman
ditch
N-S

N

V

W

W

Manorial
enclosure
wall

AA

J

Q:
Iron Age
?quarries

K Roman
ditch

F

a

a

a

L

Anglo-Saxon
SFB

T SFB

SFB

Z

S

H
Iron Age
ditch

G Iron Age
quarry
or ditch terminal

N

Roman
ditch

K

stoking
pit

Wharram
Percy

Roman
corn drying
or malting
oven

BB

T flue
phase 1

P

Medieval terraced
yard or building

R

Roman
ditch

0   10
                                    metres

PAR 1983-4

Fig. 37b

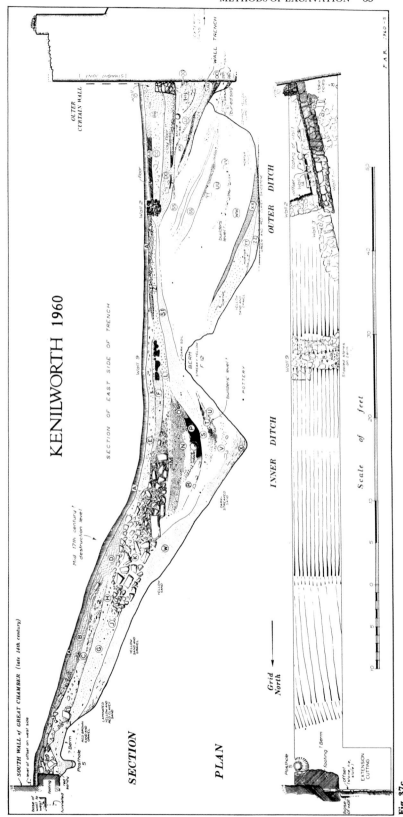

KENILWORTH 1960

SECTION OF EAST SIDE OF TRENCH

SOUTH WALL of GREAT CHAMBER (late 14th century)

Mid 17th century destruction level

SECTION

PLAN

Grid
North

Scale of feet

OUTER CURTAIN WALL

WALL TRENCH

OUTER DITCH

INNER DITCH

Fig. 37c

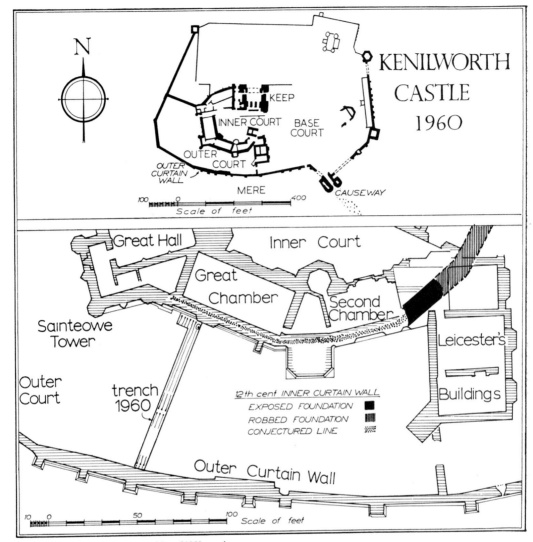

Fig. 37d   Plan of castle showing position of 1960 trench.

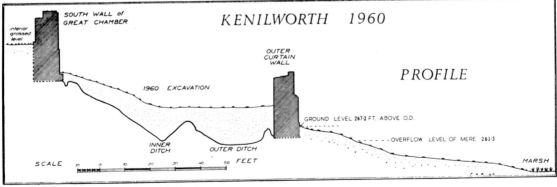

Fig. 37d   profile of section in relation to other levels.

Fig. 38

would not have revealed the long sequence of more or less parallel roads which, over many centuries, produced deep ruts and, eventually, a small valley. Although the sequence is not yet clear, it seems likely that the road was ultimately moved up on to the shoulder to the left of the picture, perhaps because of the fact that water would inevitably drain down the hollow-way, making it difficult for traffic.
(With acknowledgements to Charles Hill and Godfrey Sittig)

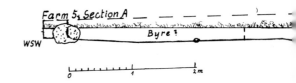

Farm 5, Section A

WSW   Byre ?

0   1   2 m

Farm 5, Section B   1m below Datum point.

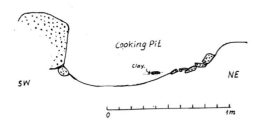

NW   Cooking Pit   Hearth Stone   SE

Clay →   ← Clay

0   1 m

Farm 5, Section C   1m below Datum point.

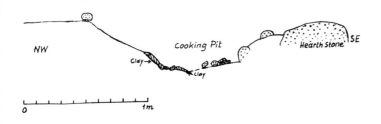

Cooking Pit

clay.

SW   NE

0   1m

Farm 5. Section E
South Facade of Cooking Pit and Hearth Stone   1m below Datum point.

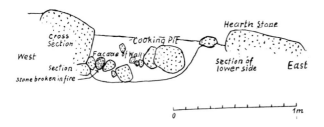

Hearth Stone

Cross
Section   Cooking Pit

West   Facade of Wall

section   Section of
lower side   East
Stone broken in fire

0   1m

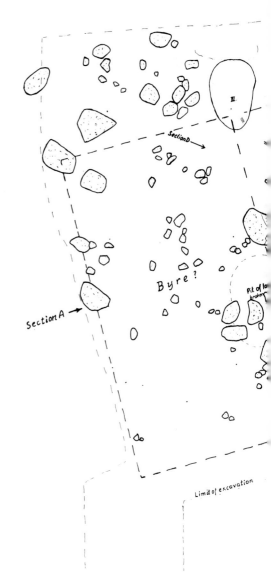

Section D →

Byre ?

Section A →

Pit of lo
broken

Limit of excavation

Fig. 39

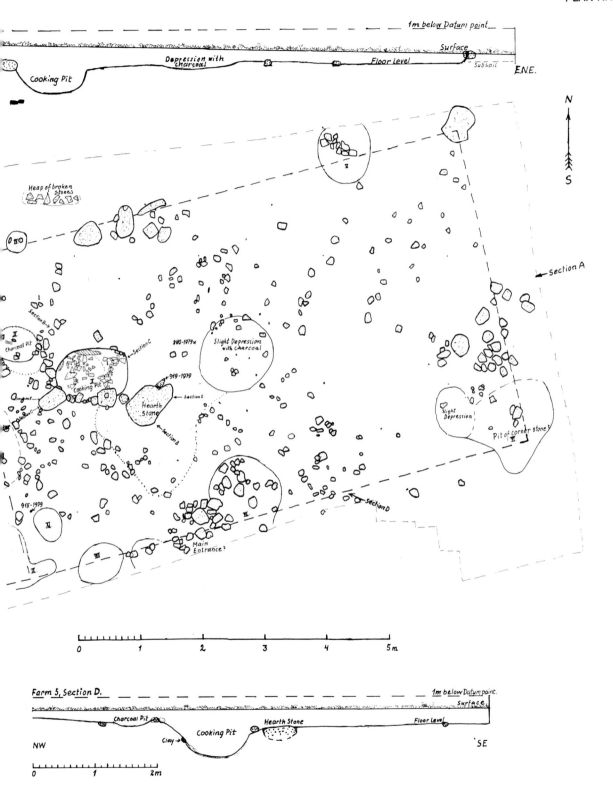

1m below Datum point

Surface

Depression with Charcoal

Floor level

Subsoil

Cooking Pit

E.N.E.

N

S

Section A

Heap of broken stones

Section B

Charcoal Pit

Section C

880-1979

Slight Depression with Charcoal

Section E

949-1979

Cooking Pit

Hearth Stone

Section B

Slight Depression

Pit of corner stone

915-1979

Main Entrance?

Section D

0   1   2   3   4   5 m

Farm 5, Section D.

1m below Datum point.

Surface

Charcoal Pit

Cooking Pit

Hearth Stone

Floor Level

Clay

NW

SE

0   1   2m

Fig. 40

Fig. 40 *The cumulative section*
Excavation of the bailey rampart of the motte and bailey castle at Hen Domen, Montgomery.

Because this castle was only ever of wood, the excavation has to be as complete as possible in order to recover the evidence of a rampart. This poses particular problems, since it is necessary to see the whole of the surface in plan (in order not to miss the slight evidence of timber structures) and at the same time to see a number of vertical sections, which will help to elucidate the sequence of ramparts and to demonstrate them in the eventual publication. This is done here by stripping off layers up to a predetermined line, drawing the visible section and then removing the layer beyond. If no separate layers can be distinguished, the rampart is lowered 5 or 10cm a time and the same procedure followed. This method produces a 'cumulative section' in which, although the excavator never sees the whole section at once, the result is a sequence of sections plus plans of all the surfaces, especially those with structural evidence, such as post-holes, in them. Other excavators prefer to leave very thin balks, or undug strips, between the areas they dig. The visible sections can then be drawn and the balks removed. Both methods have something to commend them, though the problem with leaving thin balks is that they may collapse before they have been drawn – the nature of the soil dictates the thickness of the balk that can be left with safety.
(Photo: R.A. Higham)

Fig. 39 Plan and sections of farm 5 at Borup, South Zealand, Denmark, excavated by Axel Steensberg (Steensberg, 1983). The settlement was occupied from AD 700 to 1400 and consisted of a number of farms within a very extensive field system. The buildings were founded on stone pads or simply on the surface of the ground, and often the only evidence for their existence was the presence of a hearth and charcoal-filled pits. The drawing reproduced shows the way in which sections have been drawn, based on levels taken during the excavation (rather than the drawing of observed sections, which is more customary). In this way, notional sections can be drawn anywhere across the site, though, strictly speaking, they are profiles rather than sections, since they contain no vertical detail.

A trench across the chest will give a certain amount of information about the heart and the lungs and part of the spine, but nothing at all about the brain or the kidneys, or, for that matter, the kneecaps. The only logical way to 'excavate' a body is to dissect it layer by layer, taking the skin from the muscles, the muscles from the skeleton, and so on, eventually dissecting each organ down to the nerves and tiny blood vessels which make it up. So it is with an archaeological site. It should be dissected logically from the surface down, in the way that the site dictates, layer by layer, feature by feature, down to the smallest visible unit, and sometimes beyond (for example, the mechanical or chemical analysis of deposits in order to understand their structure or their contents). However, this is not to say that sections are not useful and sometimes essential. At one extreme, the total stripping of a great linear earthwork, such as Offa's Dyke, or the ramparts of Maiden Castle, would be out of the question logistically, politically unacceptable, and hardly cost-effective. In such cases, a series of sections at critical points will provide the maximum practicably obtainable information, while, at the other end of the scale, it is helpful to section features of many sorts in order to reveal and record their structures. Some excavators attempt to get the best of both worlds by excavating in extensive areas, but leaving thin balks, or undug strips, across the site, drawing the visible faces of the balks as they proceed. The balks can be removed at any time to reveal the whole surface in plan. Others, of whom I am one, prefer the *cumulative* section, i.e. to excavate up to a pre-determined line, draw the visible section, and proceed to excavate the rest of the layer or feature (see Fig. 40). In this way one has a plan of each feature together with a section through either the whole site, or any part of it.

A method used by Scandinavian archaeologists is to level in every surface and every find, so that, theoretically, one can draw a section anywhere across the site. This is meant to overcome the problem of the siting of sections before one knows what to section. For example, in the excavation of a deserted village site, a section line might be set up across a visible house platform. When the building has been excavated and removed, it may well happen that there is a series of underlying buildings all on different alignments. Under these circumstances, using the method described above, it is possible to publish sections wherever they are desired, in order to show particular features (Fig. 39). The method is, however, very time-consuming, and the cumulative section, described above, is more commonly used.

The excavation of timber buildings poses somewhat different problems from that of stone buildings, since in most cases the timber has rotted long ago, so that, although the *methods* of excavation are similar, in that there is no special way to dig timber buildings as opposed to that used to dig stone buildings, the evidence for timber buildings usually presents itself in different ways: as negative features if the timbers have been embedded in the ground, or as very slight traces if they have simply rested on the ground. The case of waterlogged, and therefore preserved, timbers is different again, since, while the preserved timbers can hardly be missed, their recording presents special problems, as the timbers very often lie in many separate planes, needing three-dimensional recording of a different kind from that used for stone buildings, where plans and a series of elevations may be sufficient, since their planes tend to lie at right angles to one another. Stereoscopic photography, or even small-scale models, may be the most accurate way of recording such remains in a way which can be immediately 'read' and understood. Those interested in the problems of the excavation of waterlogged wood should read the reports of the excavations of the Somerset Levels, the Fens, or the Coppergate site in York (e.g. Hall, 1984).

By far the majority of all the buildings ever built were in wood, though because stone buildings leave impressive remains they have, in the past, received most of the attention; another factor is that sites with timber buildings are difficult to dig, and have often eluded crude and summary excavation. Moreover, many sites contain both stone and timber buildings, often inextricably mixed at all periods of occupation, so that the concentration in the past on a site's stone buildings often led to the evidence for the timber buildings being dug away unnoticed. The whole site must be dug in the same sensitive way if more than the bare outlines of its development are to be recovered. Even buildings which were principally of stone may have incorporated timber partitions (see Fig. 83) or outhouses or alterations. I do not believe, therefore, that there is one way to dig sites with stone buildings and another way to dig sites with timber ones.

Excavation techniques are not dependent, therefore, in my view, on the date of the site or the nature of the occupation but more on the nature of the subsoil, the depth of the deposits, and the length of time and the amount of resources available.

For example, an excavation on a stone-free site, that is, on sand or loess or some clays, can use methods impossible on one in which the evidence for structures consists chiefly of pebbles, or rubble spreads, or, in hill country, solid rock.

On a site composed of pebbles or rubble, only meticulous hand cleaning of the surfaces will reveal their patterns and structure (see, for example, Figs. 36a, 79 and 83). On stone-free soils, horizontal cleaning with machinery or hand shovels is possible. This technique, known as the *planum* method, lowers the whole site progressively, recording it at each stage as a series of horizontal sections. This method is particularly useful on sand, where, because there are no vertical sections, there are no sides to collapse, with the consequent loss of evidence, even of workers. The *planum* method has been used with spectacular success in north-west Europe, for example, at Dorestad and Wijster in Holland (Fig. 35 and van Es, 1967). It has also been used in East Anglia on clay, by Guy Beresford at Goltho and Barton Blount, in the excavation of these

Fig. 41a   The present church of Kaupanger seen from the north-west.

Excavation and analysis of a standing building: Kaupanger Church, Norway

Figs. 41a-g illustrate the analysis and excavation of a stave church at Kaupanger, north-west of Bergen in Norway. The stave churches of Norway are the remarkable survivors of a group of wooden churches, most dating from the thirteenth century. The church at Kaupanger is first mentioned, by implication, in 1183-4, though the earliest church discovered by excavation (Building I, **Fig. 41e**) was a small, post-hole structure, without any dating evidence. The second church (Building II, **Fig. 41e**), was also founded on post-holes and

was probably that which was thought to have been burnt in 1183. The third, the present church, is probably that which was built at the end of the twelfth century to replace the burnt church, and the arcade posts rest on sleeper beams instead of being ground-fast in post-holes. This church has undergone many changes during its long life – some of them drastic. In 1862 the building was given an entirely different appearance by the insertion of a great number of new windows (**Fig. 41b**).

The analysis of the standing building,

together with the complete excavation of its interior, took place between 1959 and 1965 and it was later restored to something like its seventeenth-century appearance, which itself must have been close to its medieval form. The close observation of the church produced a wealth of structural detail which enabled a reconstruction of the twelfth-century church to be drawn (**Figs. 41f** and **41g**).

The excavation revealed that there had been at least two earlier churches on the site. The plan, **Fig. 41c** shows that a very large grave-pit had been dug in the seventeenth and eighteenth centuries, destroying the whole of the central area. The evidence for the earlier churches consisted of two groups of post-holes, aligned roughly along the present arcades. The sections (**Fig. 41d**) show the relationship of the arcades to the underlying post-holes. The plans of the two earlier churches assume that they had no aisles, though it is possible that the evidence for them had been destroyed in the building of the subsequent churches, since the outer walls are of flimsier construction than the arcades, which sit on fairly massive sill.

(Drawings and photos: courtesy of Hans-Emil Liden. The work is published by the late Kristian Bjerknes and Hans-Emil Liden, *The Stave Churches of Kaupanger*, Fabritius, 1975.)

Fig. 41b In the year 1862 the church got a great number of new windows, not only in the aisles, but also in the central part of the nave.

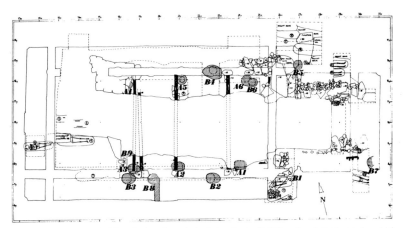

Fig. 41c *Excavation plan* The placing of post holes belonging to Buildings I and II. Post holes which belong to Building I are marked with a A and shading which slants up towards the left. Post holes and pits belonging to Building II are marked with a B and shading which slants up towards the right. The boundaries for the holes left by the actual posts are stippled in the holes were they could be observed. Stippled lines also indicate our digging boundaries and sections. The inner contours of the present church are drawn in an unbroken line.

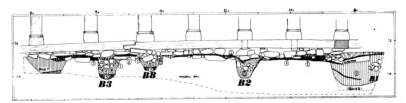

Fig. 41d Section along 7.2 y (in the southern aisle along the south side of the nave's southern raft beam). Facing south.

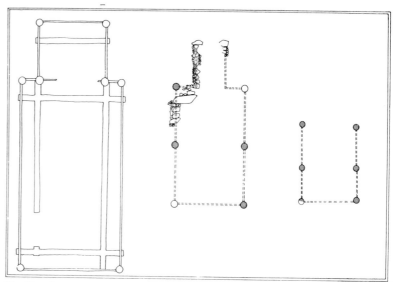

Fig. 41e   showing the proportional size of Buildings I, II and the present church. Building I to the right. Definite post holes are shaded in. Presumed lines of walls are stippled.

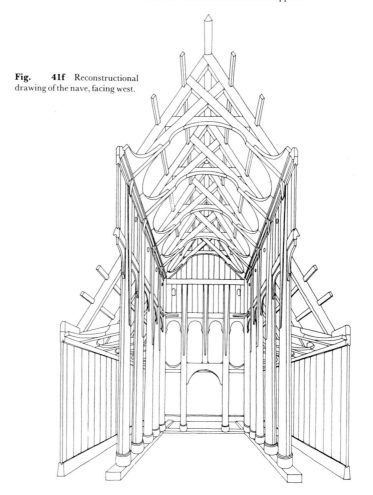

Fig.   41f Reconstructional drawing of the nave, facing west.

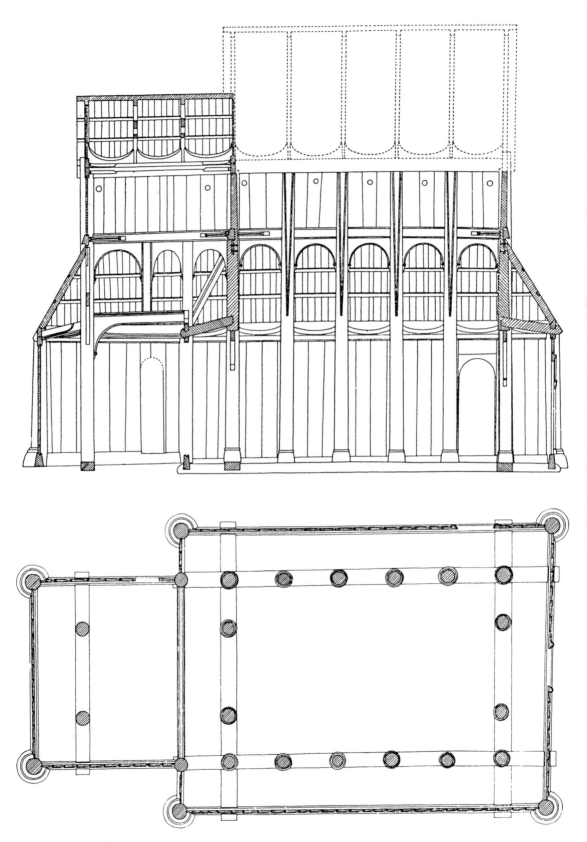

Fig. 41g Reconstruction of the original church.
Below: Ground plan. *Above:* Longitudinal section facing north.

Fig. 42a

Figs. 42a-f *Excavation and analysis of a standing building: Dudley Castle*
In parallel with the complete repair and consolidation of the castle at Dudley, West Midlands, a programme of analysis of the buildings and the excavation of the earlier phases of the castle has begun. The castle stands within the grounds of Dudley Zoo, so that there is every opportunity to show the public the work in progress – a continually changing archaeological show, which is, in my opinion, much more interesting than a site laid out in gravel and shaved grass. However, even the

excavation at Dudley will have to come to an end one day, and then the problem will be to go on presenting the castle in a lively and colourful way which will attract and hold the interest of the public at all age levels.
The excavation has started in two areas: one, the motte top, both within and outside the fourteenth-century keep (Areas 1 and 4 on **Fig. 42b**), and the other in a small, unused area between two buildings (Area 2 on **Fig. 42b**). Work is in progress on both areas, but enough has been found to justify more extensive excavation within and around the buildings. The

standing walls themselves limit the areas available for excavation, and, as can be seen, earlier walls often run underneath the present walls, showing that there have been changes in the design of the castle which can only be understood by excavation.
The photograph of Area 2 (**Fig. 42c**) shows this clearly. The photographer was standing on the curtain wall, A, looking down at the excavation (see **Fig. 42b**). After modern debris had been removed, two massive wall foundations B-B-B, were revealed. These are of a substantial building, which, from a number of linked

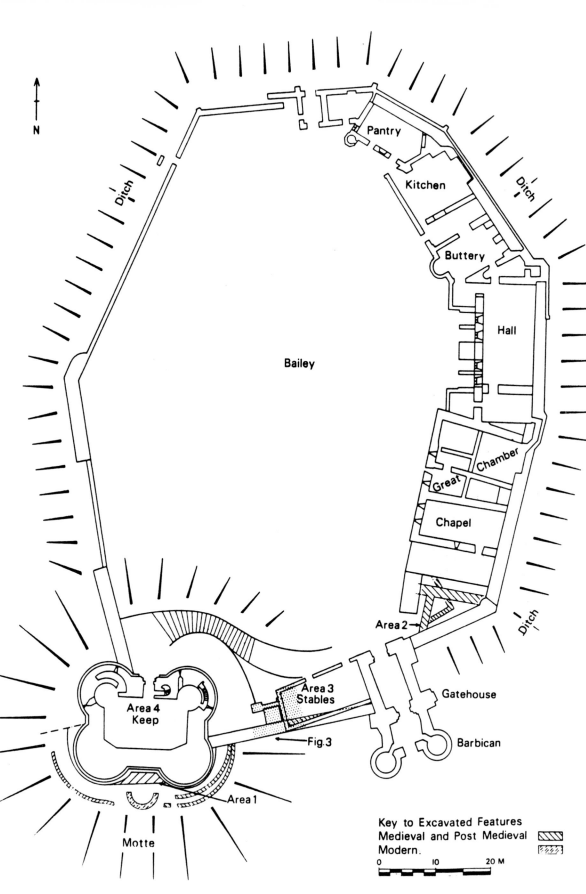

N

Ditch

Pantry

Kitchen

Ditch

Buttery

Hall

Bailey

Chamber

Great

Chapel

Area 2

Ditch

Gatehouse

Area 3
Stables

Fig. 3

Barbican

Area 4
Keep

Area 1

Motte

Key to Excavated Features
Medieval and Post Medieval
Modern.

0   10   20 M

Fig. 42b Dudley Castle. Location plan.

Fig. 42c

Fig. 42d

arguments based on evidence from pottery and the study of the nearby buildings, seem to have been part of an Elizabethan range demolished after the Civil War in 1647. Building B cut through evidence of iron-smelting which overlay an earlier building still, C-C. This is tentatively dated to the twelfth century, but excavation is continuing (1985) and there is every reason to believe that there will be earlier buildings here and elsewhere, since the earthworks of the castle are those of a motte and bailey (**Figs. 42a** and **42b**), and these almost always began with timber buildings. Even in this very small area there is clear evidence of three phases of buildings before the present, and probably more to come.

Fig. 42d is taken looking down the shell of one of the spiral staircases in the keep which crowns the motte at Dudley, showing the excavation proceeding on the floor of the interior of the keep. The surface which is visible in the **Fig. 42e** is one of the latest – the holes to be seen close to the walls being scaffold holes, presumably for repairs.

Hand in hand with the excavation, a detailed study of the standing walls is being carried out. These are being drawn stone by stone and analysed in the same way as an excavation, only in the vertical plane. **Fig. 42f** shows an example of this study. It is an elevation of one wall of a building of many periods standing at the foot of the motte. As can be seen, there is a clear indication of a blocked doorway, A. There are various other alterations and additions on the extreme right of the drawing. This is not the place to give a detailed interpretation of the elevation; it is sufficient to say that the blocked doorway probably led to a steep stair up to the motte top, and excavation in the probable stair-well on the other side of the wall not only confirms this but is adding even more phases of occupation, some unexpected, to the story. The point to be made is that detailed recording and analysis of standing structures is inseparable from their excavation, and that one illuminates the other.

(Photo: S.J. Linnane and W.D.C. Cocroft)

Fig. 42e

Stables,
West Gable End.

Fig. 42f

deserted village sites (Beresford, 1975). Clearly, waterlogged sites, such as the Somerset Levels or the Fens, will require their own adaptations of the basic techniques. Other excavations may demand a combination of many different approaches; Hen Domen, Montgomery, is one of these – horizontal excavation has been combined with cumulative, or running sections and with sections cut across linear features, such as the defensive ditches. Sometimes it has been possible to dig features entire; on other occasions they have been sectioned in quadrants, or subjected to miniature *planum* excavations. In other words, although the ideal of extensive horizontal excavation has been kept in view, it has been modified to cope with particular problems. For a more extended discussion of the methods used at Hen Domen, and the reasons for using them, see Barker and Higham, 1982.

RESEARCH, RESCUE AND SALVAGE EXCAVATIONS

Research excavations are those which are carried out on sites which are not threatened by imminent development or destruction. As a result, they can be planned without haste, and, assuming that adequate resources are available, they can be dug without haste and, most importantly, with time to think, to consider the changing problems which arise as the excavation proceeds, and to record all the evidence which can be recognized in unhurried detail.

Inevitably, since all excavation necessarily destroys the site being excavated, there has been a reaction against excavating unthreatened sites, a case put most succinctly by Olaf Olsen in *Rabies Archaeologorum* (*Antiquity*, 1980, vol. 44 pp. 15-20) in which he accuses the present writer of suffering from the nasty disease of compulsive site destruction, the mad dog of British archaeology. The writer's defence is printed in the same copy of *Antiquity*. The argument is that, since so many archaeological sites are being destroyed, our sites are a wasting asset, and therefore no unthreatened site should be dug, and the only excavations carried out should be *rescue excavations*, using all the available resources to recover as much evidence as possible from those sites which are going to be destroyed anyway, leaving unthreatened sites for posterity. This means, in effect, that archaeological strategy is dictated by the bull-dozer rather than by carefully considered research priorities. The argument used is that if threatened sites are looked on as the raw material of research, then rescue excavations can be turned into research excavations. Ultimately, after a great many sites have been excavated in this way, the results can be amalgamated into a synthesis which would be little different from that produced by a research strategy on unthreatened sites.

The difficulty lies in excavating threatened sites at the pace and with the completeness of research excavations. Another factor which tends to distort the ultimate picture is that whole categories of site are unlikely to be threatened by development. These include most motte and bailey castles, most stone castles, most major Roman forts, and most cathedrals and their precincts. For example, beneath or close to the cathedral at Worcester must lie the remains of two Anglo-Saxon minsters, and there is some evidence, from a small excavation in the recent past, that there has been a Christian community on the site since Roman times. It is most unlikely that there will be any major developments in or around the cathedral within the foreseeable future. How, then, will it be possible to throw light on, let alone solve, the questions of the cathedral in Worcester's history without excavating unthreatened sites, as was done in Winchester to reveal the plans of the Old and New Minsters in the 1960s (Biddle, 1964-70, 1972, 1975, etc.)? This situation can be paralleled in hundreds of other cases where major sites are, quite properly, protected, but are thereby sterilized from future examination.

The writer's view is that a programme of carefully considered rescue excavations, fitting in with regional, if not national, strategies, together with carefully chosen research excavations would be the best solution, both from the academic point of view and the point of view of the public, since, by definition, rescue excavations are almost always carried out on sites which are subsequently destroyed. If sites are to be properly displayed to the public, they should be thoroughly investigated (so that the most complete account of them can be given) and this presumes that they are protected sites, and that therefore any excavations on them will be in the research category.

Salvage excavations are those which are carried out in the face of the imminent destruction of the site, often no more than a watching brief while the site is being destroyed with perhaps the opportunity to clear a section by hand or to record something of the plan of a building. Under these circumstances, all the evidence must be treated with caution. The bucket of the mechanical digger will not only smear and obscure the section but may carry pottery down from near the surface and embed it in the side of the trench. Under such circumstances, it is best to rely only on dating evidence recovered by hand from unequivocally stratified contexts. Nevertheless, even salvage excavations can produce important results which otherwise might be completely lost (see Fig. 31).

THE EXCAVATION OF STANDING BUILDINGS

It is easy to think of archaeology as relating only to what is underground and unseen, but not only do standing buildings, or their ruins, have their own archaeology, but they can only properly be understood in relation to their foundations and, through them, to the strata which surround them. This can perhaps be most easily illustrated in the case of a church, perhaps built in stone for the first time in the ninth century, but replacing two earlier timber churches on the same site. The foundations of the stone building will cut through the remains of the timber structures, or, if it is larger, may completely enclose them. Graves, whether inside or outside the original church may be cut by the new foundations, and the new floors will seal the earlier remains. Eventually the stone church is likely to prove too small for an expanding congregation, and it will be enlarged, very probably incorporating parts of the earlier building. The piecemeal enlargement of the church could span many centuries and many different styles, but, under changed circumstances, the building may become redundant, and fall into ruin.

It will be clear that any study of such a church would be incomplete without excavation inside and out, and there have been some very good examples of the total study of churches, that is, of the standing structure as well as the buried evidence, both in Britain and on the Continent (see Rodwell, 1981, and here, Figs. 41a-g).

CHAPTER FIVE

Recognizing and recording the evidence

Archaeological sites are almost infinite in their variety, from Minoan palaces to palaeolithic wind-breaks. So also is the variety of evidence which is found in the ground. This may range from unmissable masonry foundations of massive size to the almost undetectable traces of a wattle and daub hut. One must add to this the immense variety of finds of all kinds – pottery, metalwork, preserved timber and leather, bones (both human and animal), and the macroscopic environmental evidence provided by seeds, twigs, leaves, snails and so on, together with the microscopic evidence of pollen, the remains of parasites, etc.

In the face of all this, the excavator must, after the lifting of the first sod, be prepared for anything. The structural evidence may present itself in one or more of a great number of ways. The known site of a large building, say a medieval manor house, may prove to have well-preserved stone foundations, or may, if it was built in the great half-timber tradition, only survive as a level area, bounded by a few pebbles. A few small post-holes and a pattern of wear on the floor of a large Roman building may be the only indication of a later structure, built when the earlier building had gone out of use.

Too often, in the past, excavators had preconceived ideas about the structures they were looking for, and so ignored other evidence which, even if it did not stare them in the face, gave them a significant glance. The excavator has, therefore, to be aware of all the varieties of evidence which might be encountered, and be very careful not to ignore evidence which inconveniently does not fit his expectations. It is difficult to be totally objective, to have a completely neutral approach to the site and its evidence – instant interpretations obtrude constantly as the site is uncovered and these have to be turned to good advantage, so that they constantly modify the questions which prompted the excavation in the first place. Nevertheless, having said this, the *recording* of the evidence must be as objective as possible, so that it can be looked at, long after the site has been destroyed, with a fresh and unbiased eye.

So, it will be seen that the immediate objectives of excavation are the recognition, and then the recording, of the evidence as it is uncovered.

The recognition includes more than simply the observation of wall foundations or rubbish pits or drainage gullies – it includes also the recovery of all the other evidence outlined above, the pottery and small finds, the environmental evidence, and every other observed phenomenon which might add to the understanding of the site. Much of this can – in fact, must – be recorded on the site, but the environmental evidence is usually sampled (see p. 70; Figs. 71a, b; Fig. 72) and recorded in detail later.

Some excavators take as objective a view as possible of the whole process, reserving any attempt at interpretation until the site has been recorded in detail, by drawing, photography and the written record. Others, myself included, believe that it is a mistake not to take every opportunity to understand the site, and that one of those opportunities is when the area under excavation is freshly revealed, since it will never be quite the same again; the weather – drying in the sun, soaking by rain, erosion by wind – will alter the newly trowelled surfaces in their various ways. Sometimes, in fact, the surfaces will reveal more after a shower has dried, or a rubble surface has been washed by heavy rain, but whether the excavated area is improved or not, it will have changed, and all these changes will add or subtract something from what can be observed. In many ways, the secret of good excavation lies in intense observation, in seeing as much as possible in the excavated surfaces or sections, and in the relationships between them, both while the excavation is proceeding and afterwards as the records are being analysed.

The excavation of the latest occupation of the Baths Basilica at Wroxeter Roman City provides a good example of the necessity for immediate observation, and also of the difficulty of recording and publishing or demonstrating all that can be observed on the spot. The layers immediately below the topsoil consisted of spreads of rubble. These were clearly different in composition and were not random. As the excavation proceeded, it was realized that the rubble spreads had been laid in rectangular areas, and there was every reason to believe that these were the foundations of timber-framed buildings, one of them of great size, whose ground-sills simply lay on the rubble platforms. There was no doubt in the minds of those of us who saw these platforms that this is what they were, and they were drawn in great detail and with as much objectivity as possible. They were also photographed vertically and stereoscopically (though in black and white, when colour would undoubtedly have been better if it had been available). The shape and character of the platforms was seen particularly clearly when one walked round the site, thus viewing them not only stereoscopically, which is our normal way of looking, but adding to this the extra 'dimension' of movement. If we watch the passing landscape from a train, the relative movement of the trees and hedgerows against one another enhances our three-dimensional understanding of the landscape. If the train stops in open country, we still see the landscape three-dimensionally, but much less clearly. The difficulty of demonstrating the subtleties of the rubble platforms at Wroxeter, which could be clearly seen when we walked round them, but which were very difficult to photograph, led to the suggestion that the video camera might be the best way of demonstrating their undoubted existence.

THE IMPORTANCE OF NEGATIVE EVIDENCE

Most of excavation consists of looking for what is left of the site, recording it in great detail and trying to make sense of it. But it is also very important to realize what is missing, what you would expect to be there but is not, and to use this negative evidence to illuminate the site's development, or, at least, to raise questions which would otherwise not have occurred had you not realized that there were gaps in the evidence. An obvious example, which could hardly have been overlooked, was the apparent lack of a body in the Sutton Hoo ship burial (Bruce-Mitford, 1975). Such a sumptuously furnished barrow must surely have commemorated the death of an important figure. If there was no body, why not? Was the mound a cenotaph to a warrior killed elsewhere, perhaps drowned and his body irrecoverable? Or was he a Christian, buried in an unfurnished grave but commemorated with a cenotaph by his pagan followers or family? Or, as now seems likely, was there a body which remained undetected by the excavators because it had almost totally decayed? The negative evidence, in this case the lack of an obvious corpse, raised a host of questions which demanded further investigation.

Two less obvious examples may be cited from Wroxeter. The Baths Basilica there was a building on the scale of a cathedral, with two colonnades with columns some 20 feet (6 metres) high and 3 feet (1 metre) in diameter. It has been estimated that the stone slates on the roof alone weighed some 2,300 tons without the massive timbers needed to support them. This great structure seems to have gone out of use as a public building around AD 300 and there is ample evidence that within its walls was built a succession of timber buildings, some of them very large, and lasting until at least AD 500. It was only gradually that we realized, as we went on excavating the evidence for the later buildings from within the basilica, that all the layers that we were removing must have been brought in from elsewhere in the city to form the foundations for the timber buildings which had subsequently filled the area. Nowhere was there the sort of debris which would be expected from a collapsed building, no massive fragments of columns, no pieces of sculptured capitals or mouldings, and only one comparatively small chunk of masonry which seemed to be lying where it fell. When a great building becomes unsafe, there are only three options – to repair it, to get out quickly before it collapses, or to demolish it. Our basilica had not been repaired, and clearly it had not simply been allowed to collapse, since if it had, it was inconceivable that the great weight of the columns and the walls would not have destroyed the floors on which they fell, embedding themselves in them. Nor would every fragment have been removed without trace from a collapsed building before its site was redeveloped. The conclusion which is inescapable is that the basilica had been deliberately dismantled, the roof removed, and the columns taken down systematically. There is evidence that the walls remained, so that for a time the site looked like that of a great kitchen garden, an open space surrounded by walls, against which, later, lean-to buildings were constructed. Earlier excavators, digging only part of the building assumed that it had simply collapsed. The evidence obtained from a much more extensive excavation showed that this could not be so, the negative evidence suggesting very strongly the hitherto unlikely theory of the basilica's dismantling.

The other example is also from Wroxeter. During the course of the excavation of the buildings of the latest occupation, the rubble platforms on which they were founded were found to contain a number of large fragments of human skulls (Fig. 43). Human bones are quite common finds from the later levels of Roman towns and have usually been ascribed to sub-Roman burials dating from the time when civic order had broken down and the old rule of burial outside the city limits had been forgotten. At Wroxeter itself, on the adjacent forum, skeletons had been found in ditches and elsewhere and were assumed to have been post-Roman in date. We might have assumed this about the skull fragments found in the latest levels of the basilica, but here we had the advantage that we had dug the whole site, and not merely trenched it. In common with most Roman sites, there were thousands of animal bones but the only human bones that we could recognize were the skull fragments. The animal bone specialist confirmed that there were no human bones among the animal bones sent for examination. This negative evidence was crucial. The skulls could not, therefore, be regarded as the remnants of complete burials but must be the remains of skulls separated from the rest of the skeleton and kept for some purpose. Many of these skull fragments had yellowish, greasy surfaces. Scientific examination of these surfaces shows that the skulls had been immersed or anointed in a yellowish vegetable oil containing linoleic acid. A number of the skulls had sword or knife cuts at their bases and one had knife cuts on the hair-line of the forehead, which strongly suggests scalping. The inescapable conclusion is that the heads had been detached from their bodies, the flesh removed and the skulls treated with oil, presumably so that they could be preserved and perhaps displayed as relics or trophies. The cult of the head is well known in the Celtic world, but it is unexpected to find evidence of it in the centre of a Roman city and at so late a date. The date of the skulls is uncertain at present but they could not have become dispersed in the rubble platforms of the last period rebuilding of the basilican area either before AD 300 (the presumed date of the basilica's destruction) or after about AD 400 ± 25, the presumed date of the rebuilding. The crucial distinction is between evidence of absence, and absence of evidence.

All excavation is destruction – when the site has been destroyed all that is left are the site records, the finds and some unreliable memories. The records must, therefore, be as full and reliable as it is possible to make them. There are three broad divisions of records – written, drawn and photographic.

THE WRITTEN RECORD

This consists of immediate on-site descriptions of layers and archaeological features (collectively called by most archaeologists 'contexts'). Over the years, various forms of record cards and sheets have been devised to ensure at least some standardisation in the recording. The advantage of the pro forma type of record is that it not only reminds the recorder of all the entries that should be made, or at least considered, but also draws attention to those elements of the context which might have been expected, but which were positively not there. This is important, because it is as vital to record negative evidence as it is positive.

An example of a recording sheet is reproduced in Fig. 44 (front) and Fig. 45 (back). A separate sheet of this sort is filled in for every recognizable feature (or context) on the site. This has been evolved for use at Wroxeter and elsewhere, and, though similar to many other such sheets, is by no means the last word, and the interested reader may like to compare it with versions from other sites.

It will be seen that the sheet illustrated, which has been taken from the site archive, has been filled in by a number of different people, as the feature was progressively worked on and recorded. There are entries of many kinds, recording the location of the feature and its reference number together with a description, kept separate from the provisional interpretation. Other entries record samples taken for analysis, plan numbers and details of a contour survey of the upper surface of the layer. In the box at the top of the reverse of the sheet is information regarding the relationship of adjacent contexts, which will be used to construct the stratification diagram or matrix (see pp. 142, 143).

It is not suggested for a moment that this sheet has been ideally completed, but it is a real example of part of the record of each context or feature.

The written record also includes finds and sample recording forms, together with less formalized notebooks, day-books, and so on, kept by the director and site supervisors to record their thoughts, however ephemeral, since these form an account of work in progress which supplements the stereotyped record.

Increasingly, also, tape recorders are being used as site notebooks, to be transcribed later into typescript, or simply to capture immediate thoughts which may be forgotten unless they are recorded. One advantage of the small note-taking type of tape recorder is that it can be carried round the site and 'chatted to' in a way impossible with a notebook.

Forms have also been devised for the recording of more specialized excavations or features, for example the form reproduced in Fig. 46 for the recording of human burials. The excavation of cemeteries is, as can be imagined, very time-consuming, since each skeleton, together with its grave goods, if any, has to be meticulously excavated and cleaned. Any way in which the recording can be speeded up is therefore extremely valuable, so that vertical photography, either in mono or stereoscopically (see p. 126) and formalized recording sheets are used whenever possible.

Readers interested in more detail should read the *Site Manual, Part 1, The Written Record* published by the Department of Urban Archaeology of the Museum of London.

As in every other field, computers are being used increasingly in archaeology, particularly for the analysis of large quantities of data, such as pottery, bone and flint, and for the plotting of a mass of readings, as in contour surveys. The increased miniaturization of computers has meant that they can now conveniently be taken on site. Dominic Powlesland, of the Heslerton Parish Survey, which is studying the evolution of the Yorkshire landscape, has pioneered the use of microprocessors in the field. Figs. 47a-i illustrate the system which he has devised and some of the results. It will be clear that the potential of these small machines is very considerable, speeding up recording, storing large quantities of data in a rapidly accessible form, and enabling a great variety of analyses to be carried out swiftly and efficiently. In addition, plans and sections can be drawn on the machine using data which has been digitized.

THE DRAWN RECORD

The drawn record of an excavation consists principally of plans of the whole or parts of the site together with plans of single features or contexts, plus sections, both across large parts of the site or of individual features, such as post-holes, pits, gullies, robber trenches, and so on. Plans of areas are commonly drawn at a scale of 1:20, while plans of small features, or features incorporating a considerable amount of detail, are drawn at 1:10, as are their sections. Some archaeologists draw each single feature or context separately, only amalgamating them later with the aid of a matrix or stratification diagram (pp. 142, 143). Others draw

[118

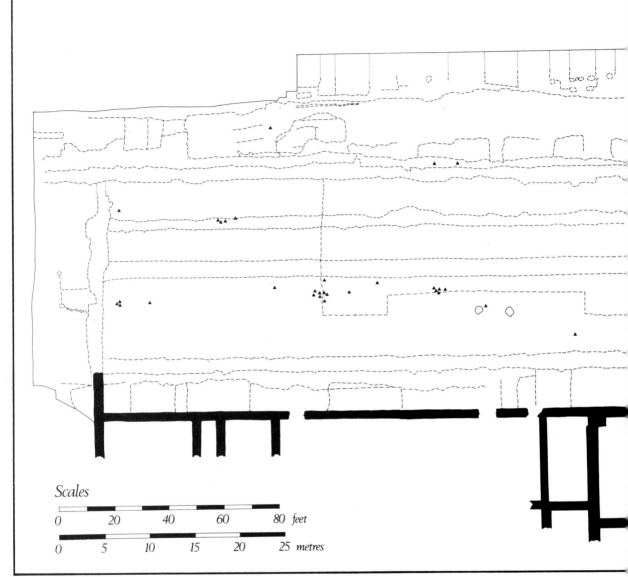

WROXETER ∘ *Baths Basilica* ∘ *Distribution of Human Skull Fragments*

Scales

| 0 | 20 | 40 | 60 | 80 *feet* |

| 0 | 5 | 10 | 15 | 20 | 25 *metres* |

Fig. 43

Fig. 43 This plan of the area of the Baths Basilica at Wroxeter shows the distribution of the human skull fragments. It is a good example of the value of careful recording of the provenance of finds *before* their importance is realized – afterwards is too late. *All* finds, therefore, have to be recorded with considerable precision if their potential is to be realized. In this case there must surely be some significance in the fact that the majority of the skull fragments come from the central part of the basilica nave. What that significance is, is not yet certain, and will depend on further post-excavation analysis, but the skulls seem to be firmly linked with this building and its use.

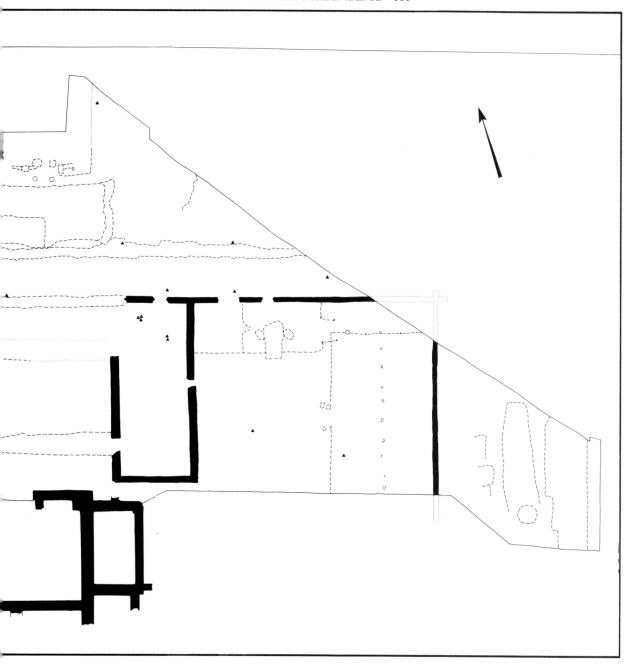

Fig. 44

Site WP | Area J | Grid 27 28 (14) | Feature 762 | Date Found 1982 | Code
Date Dug 1982

GRID REFERENCE E | N | GENERAL LOCATION
0 2 5 0 7 8 5 0 | Western portico - north of D172

DESCRIPTION Dark brown silt (30) fine sand (70) (Munsell wet 7.5YR 3/2), small patches yellower colour towards south, later patches towards south-east, including moderate quantity flecks orange red brick/tile, occasional small frag red sandstone tile & medium + small river worn pebbles, fleck charcoal, animal bone (including 3 skulls articulated + unbroken) occupies generally thin skins especially towards north and west (where present crudely lying with stones + pebbles) and under D462. Patchy burnt orange silt overlying thin skins distinct approx 0.20m diam. occurs as lens 0.02-0.03m thick within D762 at approx (25) 96004200 (level PTO). Burnt clay.

INTERPRETATION Either dump or very rapid accumulation on top of pebble and similar surfaces (D928 etc). Large unbroken bones argue against use as surface or lengthy deposition (photographed) lying on the surface of underlying D928 under reference to D928).

POST-EXCAVATION RELIABILITY

METHOD OF EXCAVATION trowel
METHOD OF COLLECTION OF FINDS normal
TYPES OF FINDS PRESENT BUT NOT COLLECTED
RISK OF CONTAMINATION LOW | AVERAGE ✓ | HIGH
SAMPLES SS 112 109 104 C14 sample of charcoal from Eq110N6CCC.
SPECIAL FINDS

PLAN NOS 14/2/5, 13/1/6, 27/3/8, 28/4/5, 28/2/5, 27/1/4
SECTION NOS | OTHER DRAWINGS
PHOTOGRAPHS: B.W. NEGS Sydney 1982 | B.W. PRINTS
COLOUR SLIDES | PRINTS | VERTICAL SURFACE

Fig. 45

STRATIFICATION | LOCALISED MATRIX SHEET NO.
UNDERLIES 763 462 766 711
OVERLIES 928
CUTS
CUT BY 96 871 872 873
ABUTS
EQUALS
OTHER

PHOTOGRAPHS AND/OR CONTINUATION
levels
burnt clay TBM 61.190 BS 1.440 FS 1.920
D762 underlying D462 TBM 61.190 BS 1.440 FS 1.970

Contour survey

1.	60.635	11.	60.675	21.	60.625	31.	60.510	41.	60.085
2.	60.705	12.	60.685	22.	60.670	32.	60.595	42.	60.635
3.	60.710	13.	60.685	23.	60.685	33.	60.650	43.	60.705
4.	60.710	14.	60.700	24.	60.750	34.	60.695	44.	60.805
5.	60.760	15.	60.770	25.	60.800	35.	60.790	45.	60.810
6.	60.690	16.	60.665	26.	60.685	36.	60.625	46.	60.640
7.	60.735	17.	60.65	27.	60.625	37.	60.595	47.	60.750
8.	60.700	18.	60.70	28.	60.650	38.	60.760	48.	60.790
9.	60.705	19.	60.730	29.	60.690	39.	60.705	49.	60.680
10.	60.735	20.	60.760	30.	60.780	40.	60.765	50.	60.750

NB levels 1-45 are at 1m intervals beginning at E1m N15m in transects of 4m West to East. 46, 47 are not on transect NO at E8m 9m 10m. E7m and 8m are within the DDF pit and were not taken. Spot heights were taken at E90m N53m and E1m N53m. levels were also taken on the 2/E transects on the eastern edge of the context above the portico chisel to roller bench. These readings were used in the contour survey, but were lost before they could be recorded on this sheet.

Fig. 46

SKELETON RECORDING SHEET

Provisional Date 13-14 thc. | Type Skeleton | Site Code ABC 82 | Context 96

Grave Type Skeleton lying on layer of crushed chalk and mortar 107.

Field Diagram:

Grave Fills 94, 95 | Alignment W/E | Facing E
Grave Cut 112 | Site Grid Refs 116/236
Levels (tick) when taken ✓
Description: Incomplete articulated skeleton in prone position with surviving R lower arm crossed over chest. Head, L side and feet removed by later graves.

Treatment PVA

Stratigraphically Earlier than 95 | Stratigraphically Later than 107
Physical Relationships: ? part of family group - see skeletons 119, 126.

Samples 107 14
Special Finds
Plan Nos P 209 | Other Drawings S 19
Location on Matrix Square B2
Photographs (tick when taken) ✓ | Card Nos. 301, 302
Phase 4 | Initials and Date JR 27/2/82 | Checked by and Date R.K. 28.2.82

MUS 5004

DEPARTMENT OF URBAN ARCHAEOLOGY

```
DATA PROCESSING AT HESLERTON
COLLECTED USING PC1500
IN THE FIELD        USING PC5000 PORTABLE
                    ┌─────────────────────┐    ┌──────────────────────────────────┐
1 Context Records   │ Records Edited, Verified │  │ REPORT STAGE                      │
2 Object Records    │ saved on Bubble Memory   │  │                                  │
3 Finds Register    │ cartridges and printed   │  │ Report prepared using word-processing │
4 Samples Register  │ for inclusion in notebook │  │ package and spreadsheet package for   │
5 Survey Data       │ Catalogues printed,      │  │ generating tables.                │
                    │ primary analysis performed │  │ Data from excavation database passed │
                    └─────────────────────┘    │ directly into both packages.      │
                                               │ Plots prepared at a variety of scales │
COLLECTED OFF-SITE USING                       │ using both a commercial package and   │
MZ5600 DESK-TOP COMPUTER    POST-EXCAVATION    │ plot/chart drawing routines within │
                           ┌──────────────────┐ │ the database package.             │
1 Contexts Digitized       │ DATA SAVED ON     │ │                                  │
2 Air Photos Digitized     │ MZ5600 HARD DISK  │ │ Printed records and indexes stored both │
3 Continuation Sheets      │ BACKUP COPY ON    │ │ with the archive in the museum and │
  [additional text and     │ FLOPPY DISK.      │ │ as part of the County Council archives. │
  relationships recorded]  │ ALL RECORDS INDEXED │ │                                  │
4 Photographic Catalogue   │ CROSS REFERENCED AND │ │ Complete set of data passed back to │
5 Drawing Catalogue        │ PRINTED AFTER FINAL │ │ PC5000 disks for storage in IBM format for │
6 Specialist Data          │ CHECKING AND      │ │ use by future researchers         │
                           │ EDITING           │ │                                  │
                           │ EXTRACT RECORDS USED │ │ Data transferred to County Council │
COLLECTED ON MAINFRAME     │ FOR ANALYSIS AND  │ │ mainframe computer as part of SMR. │
                           │ GRAPHICS OUTPUT USING │ └──────────────────────────────────┘
1 SMR DATA                 │ PLOTTING AND CHART │
2 COUNTY AIR PHOTO DATA    │ GENERATING SOFTWARE │
                           └──────────────────┘
```

Fig. 47a

Fig. 47a The recording and data processing system developed by Dominic Powlesland and used in the Heslerton Parish Project for archaeological research into the evolution of the Yorkshire landscape.

Fig. 47b Dominic Powlesland recording contexts in the field using a Sharp PC 1500A.
(Photo: D.B. Wakely)

Fig. 47b

```
CODES USED IN DIGGYDO ARCHAEOLOGICAL DATABASE PACKAGE:
For use with DIGI500 DATA COLLECTION PROGRAMS on the Sharp PC5000 & PC1500
For use by HESLERTON PARISH    Project North Yorks.    England

CONTEXT Codes for CONTEXT TYPE           at 13:57:47 on 05-03-1985

1=SKELETON          2=LAYER              3=SPIT                4=FLOOR LAYER
5=GRAVEL LAYER      6=COBBLE LAYER       7=PAVEMENT            8=SOIL HEARTH
9=STONE HEARTH     10=BRK/TL. HEARTH    11=DESTRUCTION LAYER  12=ALLUVIAL LAYER
13=COLLUVIAL LAYER 14=AEOLIAN LAYER     15=REDEP. NATURAL     16=BURIED SOIL
17=DRAIN FILL      18=WELL FILL         19=COFFIN FILL        20=GRAVE FILL
21=DITCH FILL      22=PIT FILL          23=POST HOLE FILL     24=SLOT FILL
25=GULLY FILL      26=POST PIPE FILL    27=ROBBER TR. FILL    28=GRUB FILL
29=STREAM FILL     30=PLOUGH MK. FILL   31=WHEEL RUT FILL     32=STREAM F. SEG
33=GRIDDED SPIT    34=STAKEHOLE FILL    35=TRACK FILL         36=
37=               38=                  39=TRACK F. SEG        40=DITCH F. SEG
41=CREMATION      42=ARTIFACT/S        43=                   44=GULLY F. SEG
45=VOID           46=                  47=?NAT FILL          48=UNDEF FILL
49=ANIMAL HOLE FILL 50=GRAVE CUT       51=DITCH CUT          52=PIT CUT
53=POST HOLE CUT  54=SLOT CUT          55=GULLY CUT          56=POST PIPE CUT
57=ROBBER TR. CUT 58=GRUB CUT          59=STREAM CUT         60=PLOUGH MK. CUT
61=WHEEL RUT CUT  62=WELL CUT          63=                   64=STAKEHOLE CUT
65=               66=                  67=                   68=
69=               70=DITCH C. SEG      71=                   72=STREAM C. SEG
73=               74=GULLY C. SEG      75=TRACK CUT          76=
77=               78=                  79=TRACK C. SEG       80=LINED PIT
81=LINED DRAIN    82=POTTERY VESSEL    83=COFFIN GHOST       84=COFFIN
85=               86=                  87=                   88=
89=               90=                  91=                   92=
93=               94=                  95=                   96=STRUCTURE
97=?NAT CUT       98=UNDEF CUT         99=ANIMAL HOLE        100=No. Entry
```

Fig. 47c

Fig. 47c

Fig. 47c List of codes used in the Diggydo [sic] Archaeological Database Package, as printed in the field.

```
Site 20 ACContext 00082  Type DITCH C. SEG          Shape LINEAR SEG   REC. 1
Per.No Entry        L.*240 B.*210 D.***0 Grid.R. 703460/714300  Level 00000
profile UNCLEAR                           Cuts 00104        Filled by00083
+00100  +00102  +00130  000000  000000  000000  000000
CUT OF PARTIALLY EXCAVATED N-S DITCH AT E END OF TRENCH.TO E OF SEGMENT(E).WELL
DEFINED AT TOP(SPIT(73)).APPEARS TO CUT E-W BOUNDARY-100.102.104.106.
N.Plan. Y ||  D.Plan. N ||  Section N ||  C.Photo.N ||  N.Photo.N ||  Video N ||
Pottery N ||  An.Os.N  ||  Hum.Os.N ||  Objects N ||  Bld.Deb.N ||  Other N ||
C/14 N ||     Seed N   ||  Pollen N ||  Snail N ||  Organic N ||  CONTINUATION N ||
Recorded by DVP on 14  9  84    Method SH.SCRAPED Qual.ROOTED Stat.NN
```

```
Site 20 ACContext 00083  Type DITCH F. SEG          Shape LINEAR SEG   REC. 2
Per.No Entry        L.*240 B.*210 D.***5 Grid.R. 703460/714300  Level 02960
profile FLAT        Soil. SANDY SILTY LOAM Tex.MEDIUM SANDY    Mun. 10/YR/33
Fill of00082              Sealed by00001
000000  000000  000000  000000  000000  000000  000000
UPPER FILL OF PARTIALLY EXCAVATED N-S DITCH.TO THEE OF DITCH SEGMENT(E).LAYER NC
T FULLY EXCAVATED.ABUNDANT FINDS.SOME INCLUDED IN SPIT(73)commonGRAVEL
```

```
Site 20 ACContext 00100  Type DITCH CUT            Shape LINEAR        REC. 3
Per.IRON AGE        L.1205 B.**97 D.**52 Grid.R. 702612/714365  Level 02926
profile WIDE U                            Cuts 00099        Filled by00000
-00102  -00118  -00116  -00112  -00108  -00095  000000
MASTER PHASE 1 OF E-W BOUNDARY RUNNING ALONG AND ALMOST PARALLEL TO THE TRENCH.B
ASE AND SIDES CUT INTO NATURAL.FULL PROFILE EVIDENT IN E-MOST SEGMENT.
```

```
Site 20 ACContext 00102  Type DITCH CUT            Shape LINEAR        REC. 4
Per.IRON AGE        L.2590 B.**35 D.**52 Grid.R. 701930/714350  Level 02929
profile UNCLEAR                           Cuts 00100        Filled by00000
-00104  -00064  -00004  -00130  +00091  000000  000000
MASTER PHASE 2 OF E-W BOUNDARY RUNNING ALONG THE TRENCH.CUT AWAY BY PHASES 2a AN
D 3.LEAVING A LONG LEDGE IN THE NATURAL.WELL DEFINED ONLY TO THE NORTH
```

Fig. 47d

Fig. 47d Context record abstract as printed on PC 5000 in the field.

Fig. 47e Dumping records from the hand-held computer into a Sharp PC Portable Computer for printing and mass storage.
(Photo: D.B. Wakeley)

Fig. 47e

Fig. 47f Dominic Powlesland working on a grave plan using a computer aided design package. The resulting plan is reproduced in Fig. 47g.
(Photo: D.B. Wakeley)

Fig. 47f

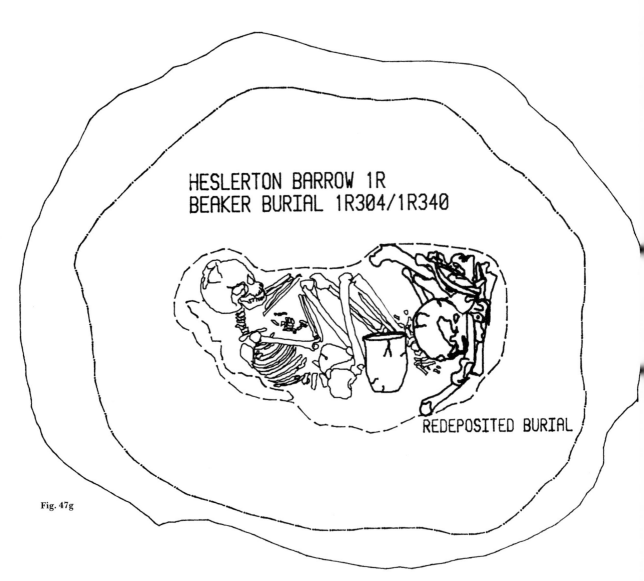

HESLERTON BARROW 1R
BEAKER BURIAL 1R304/1R340

REDEPOSITED BURIAL

Fig. 47g

Fig. 47g   Plot of an early Bronze Age burial, digitized and drawn using the Sharp Electrical Technical Drawing System.

```
Rec. No.  7  = Site 20 AA Obj.00064AC PEBBLES
Rec. No.  8  = Site 20 AA Obj.00064AD SHERD        DOMESTIC
Rec. No.  9  = Site 20 AA Obj.00064AE SHERDS       DOMESTIC
Rec. No. 10  = Site 20 AA Obj.00064AF SHERDS       DOMESTIC
Rec. No. 11  = Site 20 AA Obj.00064AG SHERDS
Rec. No. 12  = Site 20 AA Obj.00064AH SHERD        MORTARILY
Rec. No. 13  = Site 20 AA Obj.00064AI SHERD


Rec. No. 14  = Site 20 AA Obj.00064AJ SHERDS
Rec. No. 15  = Site 20 AA Obj.00064AK SHERDS
Rec. No. 16  = Site 20 AA Obj.00052AC SHERDS
Rec. No. 17  = Site 20 AA Obj.00052AD PEBBLES
Rec. No. 18  = Site 20 AA Obj.00052AE SHERD
Rec. No. 19  = Site 20 AA Obj.00052AF SHERDS
Rec. No. 20  = Site 20 AA Obj.00052AG BONES+TEETH


Rec. No. 21  = Site 20 AA Obj.00052AH SHERD        TRIPOD BASE
Rec. No. 22  = Site 20 AA Obj.00052AI SHERDS
Rec. No. 23  = Site 20 AA Obj.00052AJ SHERDS       DOMESTIC
Rec. No. 24  = Site 20 AA Obj.00052AK SHERD        DOMESTIC
Rec. No. 25  = Site 20 AA Obj.00052AL SHERD        DOMESTIC
Rec. No. 26  = Site 20 AA Obj.00069AB SHERDS
Rec. No. 27  = Site 20 AA Obj.00069AC SHERDS


Rec. No. 28  = Site 20 AA Obj.00069AD PEBBLE       ?WORKED
Rec. No. 29  = Site 20 AA Obj.00069AE PEBBLES
Rec. No. 30  = Site 20 AA Obj.00069AF SHERD        DOMESTIC
Rec. No. 31  = Site 20 AA Obj.00069AG SHERDS       DOMESTIC
Rec. No. 32  = Site 20 AA Obj.00069AH SHERD        DOMESTIC
Rec. No. 33  = Site 20 AA Obj.00069AI SHERD        DOMESTIC
Rec. No. 34  = Site 20 AA Obj.00069AJ SHERDS       DOMESTIC


Rec. No. 35  = Site 20 AA Obj.00069AK BONES+TEETH
Rec. No. 36  = Site 20 AA Obj.00073AA BONE
Rec. No. 37  = Site 20 AA Obj.00073AB PEBBLE
Rec. No. 38  = Site 20 AA Obj.00073AC BONES+TEETH
Rec. No. 39  = Site 20 AA Obj.00073AD PEBBLE       SANDSTONE
Rec. No. 40  = Site 20 AA Obj.00073AE SHERDS
Rec. No. 41  = Site 20 AA Obj.00073AF PEBBLES


Rec. No. 42  = Site 20 AA Obj.00073AG SHERD
Rec. No. 43  = Site 20 AA Obj.00073AH SHERDS
Rec. No. 44  = Site 20 AA Obj.00073AI SHERD        DOMESTIC
Rec. No. 45  = Site 20 AA Obj.00073AJ SHERD        DOMESTIC
Rec. No. 46  = Site 20 AA Obj.00073AK SHERDS       DOMESTIC
Rec. No. 47  = Site 20 AA Obj.00031AA BONES
Rec. No. 48  = Site 20 AA Obj.00031AB TEETH+BONES


Rec. No. 49  = Site 20 AA Obj.00031AC SHERDS
Rec. No. 50  = Site 20 AA Obj.00031AD SHERDS       DOMESTIC
Rec. No. 51  = Site 20 AA Obj.00031AE PEBBLE
Rec. No. 52  = Site 20 AA Obj.00031AF CALCITE LUMP
Rec. No. 53  = Site 20 AA Obj.00042AA SHERD        DOMESTIC
Rec. No. 54  = Site 20 AA Obj.00042AB TOOTH+BONE
Rec. No. 55  = Site 20 AA Obj.00042AC SHERDS       DOMESTIC
```

Fig. 47h

Fig. 47h   Finds catalogue as printed in the field on PC 5000.

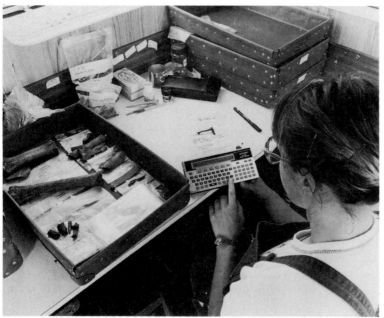

Fig. 47i

Fig. 47i   Elspeth Watson of the Heslerton Project processing finds using a Sharp PC 1500.
(Photo: D.B. Wakeley)

larger areas or phases on one sheet. The argument against this is that it is not always possible to know what is of one phase and what of another, either later or earlier, before the post-excavation analysis has taken place, so that it is important not to pre-empt that analysis. Many excavators, including the writer, adopt a less rigid approach which amalgamates both methods.

Plans, usually on plastic drawing film, are often coloured in a key, standardized for the site, which is used to distinguish types of stone tile, mortar or plaster, or the colours of the subsoil or the fillings of features. There is no generally agreed code of colours because sites are so varied, each calling for its own series of distinguishing colours or keys.

If the drawings are made to a uniform size and scale they can be joined together, if necessary over large areas – theoretically one could have a plan of every detail of a large site at 1:20. All that would be needed would be a big enough wall. The drawings must, of course, be cross-referred to the written record and the photographs, so that together they make a unity which goes a long way towards preserving the destroyed site in great detail, and in a variety of ways, each complementing the other.

THE PHOTOGRAPHIC RECORD

Photography and drawing go together to illustrate the written record – drawings, in general, are two-dimensional (though see Fig. 50a), embody accurate measurements and can delineate features and layers in a very precise way, emphasizing and selecting, if necessary. Photography has the virtues of speed; varied lighting, which can emphasize shape and surface textures, and natural colour both in prints and transparencies; it can be oblique, vertical or stereoscopic.

Oblique photography gives a good impression of what the site or any part of it 'looked like' compared with the formality of drawn plans and sections (Figs. 14, 34b, 38 and 83a). It is useful for showing relationships (Fig. 80) or, by using a low view-point or varied lighting, revealing different aspects of the subject (Figs. 51, 55, 56). Vertical photography has the advantage of being closer to the drawn plan and can therefore be used to supplement it, either in single shots (Fig. 58) or stereoscopically by a grid of overlapping photographs, in black and white or colour (Fig. 57). Photography can, therefore, provide an invaluable and objective record of each surface or feature and can be used by the draughtsman as a check on accuracy, especially if vertical photographs are enlarged to the same scale as the plans, when they can be slid under them, using a light-box, to check them and add detail. At Wroxeter, we have developed an accelerated method of recording in which outline drawings are supplemented by means of an overlapping grid of vertical colour prints, enlarged to the same scale. If the centre only of the print is used, optical distortion is reduced to a minimum.

Because of its swiftness, a series of photographs can also be used to

[*127*

Fig. 48 One of the quickest and most accurate ways of drawing the plan of the site is with the aid of a drawing frame, in this case a metre square, with strings at 20cm intervals. The draughtswoman is drawing the site at a scale of 1:20 on a board small enough to be held all day without being tiring and not liable to be blown about in strong winds. She is standing within the frame in order for her head to be vertically above the point she is drawing. One example of the sort of drawing that results is seen in Fig. 49.

Fig. 48

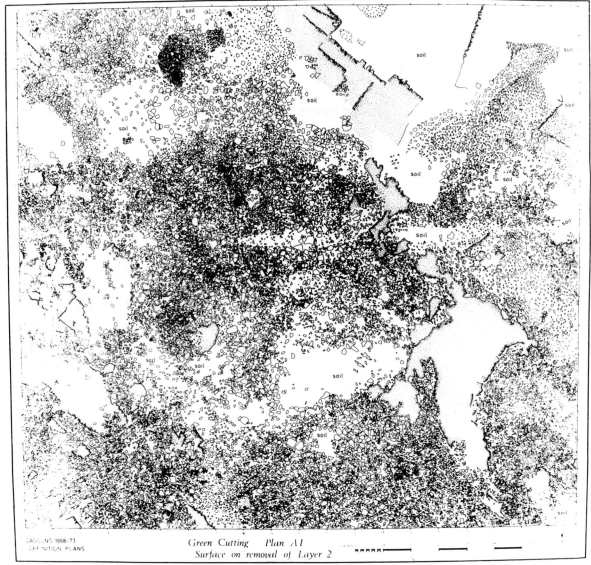

CADBURY 1968-73
DEFINITION PLANS

Green Cutting   Plan A1
Surface on removal of Layer 2

Fig. 49

Fig. 49 *Cadbury Congresbury: plan of entrance area*
This shows the stone by stone drawing (originally drawn at 1:20) of the first surface cleaned after the turf and topsoil have been removed. The stones are the upper levels of layers and features comprising the entrance of a sixth-century hillfort. It is an objective drawing without any attempt at interpretation at this stage. All subsequent plans of this area at lower levels will be subjective, as they will be drawings of those stones which the excavator has isolated by selective removal (i.e. dissection) of the stones of the latest surface (shown here). Any competent team can reach the stage of excavation represented by this drawing. It is the subsequent selective removal, dissection, and further drawing which demands experience, skill, flair, and not a little courage! (The linear area of deeper soil crossing the middle of the drawing is a post-medieval path.)
(Drawing: courtesy of Philip Rahtz)

Fig. 50a

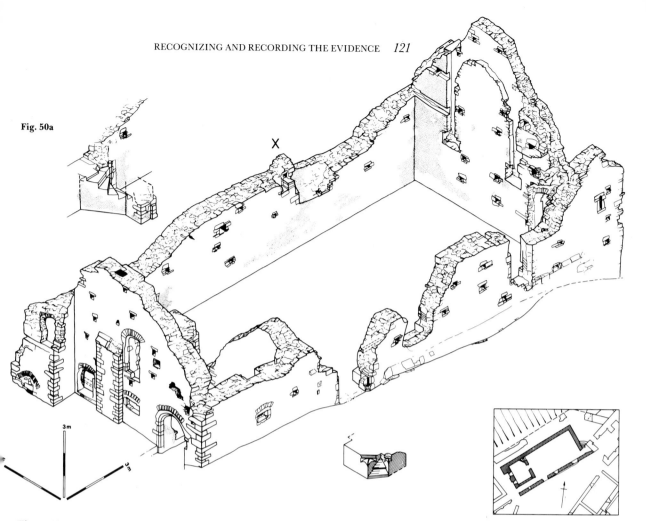

Fig. 50a shows an axonometric drawing of the great hall at Okehampton Castle, in Devon. In this form of drawing, the measurements can be scaled off correctly along three axes – those shown in the bottom left-hand corner of the figure. The viewpoint from which the drawing is made is chosen to give the maximum information, and the result is a little like an aerial view, except that it is not, of course, in perspective. Specially printed sectional paper is used to construct the drawing, which can be made on the spot, as **Fig. 50b** shows. Here the draughtsman's assistant supplies the measurements, while the draughtsman plots them directly on to the developing drawing. The part being drawn in the photograph is marked X on the drawing.
(With acknowledgements to R.A. Higham, J.P. Allan and S. Goddard)

Fig. 50b

Fig. 51

Fig. 51 The advantages of low-level lighting have been seen in the way in which it revealed the ridge and furrow at Hen Domen, Montgomery (Fig. 29a). There it was glancing sunshine; here, at Sutton Hoo, artificial light, by courtesy of the BBC, reveals features not otherwise easily seen. In the foreground is an earlier archaeological trench, in the middle ground a medieval road, and in the background the site Portacabin. This is part of the comprehensive scheme of pre-excavation examination which is being carried out as the first phase of the new campaign of research at Sutton Hoo (see Bibliography under *Sutton Hoo*).
(Photo: courtesy of Martin Carver).

Fig. 52

Fig. 52 There are more ways than one of taking vertical and high-level oblique photographs! The quadru-pod, on the extreme right, is for vertical photography, the rest for obliques. Examples of vertical photographs taken with the quadrupod can be seen in Figs. 57 and 58.

Figs. **53a** and **54a** These two photographs show the advantage of a high viewpoint when taking oblique photographs. Both are of part of the bailey of the timber castle at Hen Domen, Montgomery, and show post-hole buildings mainly of the twelfth century (see Barker and Higham, 1982 for details). The value of the figure standing in the centre of **Fig. 53a** is that she provides the structures with a scale in human terms – ranging rods, such as that in **Fig. 54a**, give a less immediately recognizable scale, especially now that metric scales of measurement are used, since ranging rods and other scales have no agreed divisions.

The two plans (**Figs. 53b** and **54b**) are of the areas shown in the corresponding photographs.

Fig. 53a

Ditch

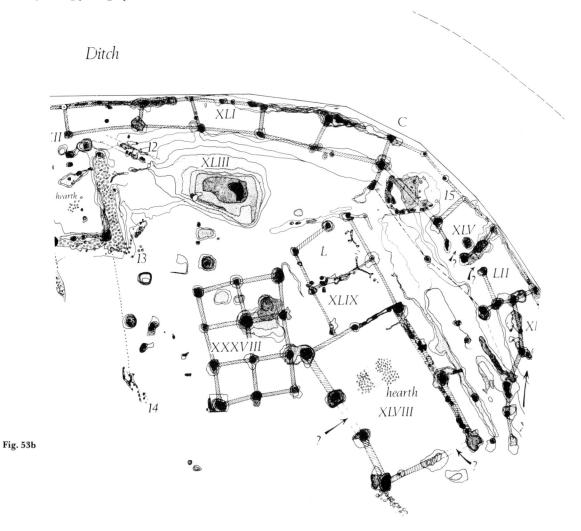

Fig. 53b

Fig. 54a

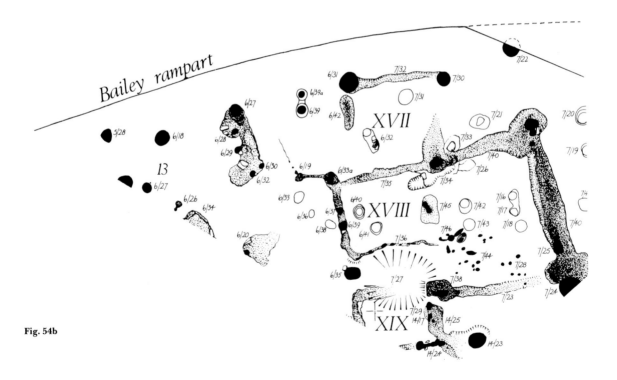

Fig. 54b

Fig. 55

Fig. 56

Figs. 55 and **56**   *Lighting*
In **Fig. 55** the photograph has deliberately been taken against the light to show the worn stone surface leading to the threshold stone of the basilica. Such a surface is very difficult to draw convincingly.

In **Fig. 56** side-lighting emphasizes the relief and shows clearly the stone drain or conduit which ran the length of the portico. Both examples from Wroxeter.
(Photo: Sidney Renow)

Fig. 57

WP83 G25 1162

Fig. 58

Fig. 57 Vertical stereoscopic view of a group of stakeholes (at top), a vertically-standing stone and part of an archaeological trench in the northern portico of the Baths Basilica at Wroxeter.
This pair of photographs can be viewed stereoscopically with a simple hand-viewer.
(Photo: Sidney Renow)

Fig. 58 A swift and accurate way of recording a burial is by vertical photography. This is a photograph of a new-born baby buried within the runis of the Baths Basilica at Wroxeter in late Roman times.
(Photo: Sidney Renow)

record the stages by which a complex feature, such as an oven or a cistern, is excavated, without appreciably holding up the work. In this respect, Polaroid cameras, with their instant results, are useful, as they can be annotated on the spot – a form of visual notebook. Photographs are also, of course, essential for the illustration of the various levels of publication and for museum displays of the results, just as slides are essential for the talks and lectures which are one of the chief ways in which the public hears about archaeology.

With the increasing availability of cameras, video recordings of excavations are becoming more and more common. They are used to record not only the formal aspects of the site, but also the enjoyments and miseries of excavation; video films are also an excellent way of bringing archaeology to a wide public on whose support the discipline ultimately depends.

FINDS

The term 'finds' covers all the portable objects which are found, from fragments of sculpture to pins and beads. They can be classified in two principle ways: either by the materials in which they are made – bone pins, combs, gaming counters; bronze pins, brooches, buckles, book-clasps; flint knives, scrapers, point, cores, flakes; iron arrowheads, nails, knives, spearheads, and so on – or by their function (since, for example, hair pins can be made of bone, iron, or bronze) as weapons, dress ornaments, tools, etc. 'Finds' do not usually include pottery, human and animal bones or coins, all of which tend to be treated separately.

Just as features or contexts are recorded on pro formas, so, usually, are finds. These are often in a form which can be used directly by the museum to which the finds are eventually going.

Allied with the recording of the finds is their conservation. In some cases, particularly those of iron and bronze objects, first-aid treatment on site is usually necessary to stop rapid deterioration. Other finds merely require careful cleaning, either dry or with water; coins are often treated on site with a fine vibrating needle or glass-fibre brush so that their inscriptions can be read, especially by those excavators who want to use them for dating – always remembering that they only give a *terminus post quem* . . .

All finds have to be packed carefully in order to avoid damage, and they can be kept dry by the addition of silica gel to the packing. In general, finds are best kept in the environment in which they were found – in other words, waterlogged finds are kept wet, and dry finds, such as those from under the floors of churches, as dry as possible. This is because over the centuries during which they have been buried they have reached a very slowly changing equilibrium with their immediate surroundings, so that, if this is maintained, their deterioration will not be accelerated, as it would be from a drastic change of environment. The most delicate objects have to go as quickly as possible to a laboratory for specialized treatment before they deteriorate irreversibly.

If finds are to yield their true potential of information they have to be recorded three-dimensionally so that, in theory at least, they can be put back precisely in the spot from which they came. Their distribution throughout the site can then be plotted and analysed, when patterns, if any, will be revealed. This detailed recording applies equally to pottery, bones (both human and animal), coins, wall-plaster, and any other category of object or building material whose distribution might be thought to be significant. Needless to say, all this takes a great deal of time, but it is essential if a great deal of information vital to the understanding of the site is not to be discarded. As in all aspects of excavation, it is one thing to recognize a pattern and another to understand what that pattern means. Sometimes the significance of a pattern of distribution will be evident – more cooking pot-sherds in the kitchen area of a castle, more glazed jug-sherds in the area of the hall and private chambers. More often, the patterns are less easily explained, partly because people don't discard or lose things or break them only where they use them, partly because on most sites there has been a good deal of earth movement, such as pit digging, foundation laying, the making-up of levels, the manuring of the ground from rubbish heaps, and so on, and, at least as much, because we simply have no way of knowing the significance, for their owners, of many of the objects, or bits of objects, that we find. One of the most salutary lessons in interpretation and its pitfalls was demonstrated by archaeologists who examined an Indian trappers' camp in Canada which had just been abandoned by its inhabitants. The archaeologists made a detailed plan of the camp and plotted all the finds – 177 bits of 'rubbish' ranging from a Dinky-toy Land Rover and a Kodak film wrapper to plastic hair curlers and a label from a pair of jeans. The archaeologists interpreted the camp on the basis of their experience, wrote a report on it and the life-style, religion, technology and economy of the people who lived there. Luckily, one of them, named Millie, was at hand to tell them the real interpretation of what they had so carefully recorded – with some amusement, because, needless to say, the archaeologists had been wrong in almost every respect (see Bonnischen, 1973, for the whole story). So it is likely that our interpretation of our finds will always be distorted by the fact that we can hardly help seeing them from our twentieth-century point of view. Philip Rahtz, in his highly entertaining *Invitation to Archaeology*, 1985, describes how, in one African society, patterns of the distribution of artifacts may be 'derived from more subtle cosmological beliefs' rather than be wholly functional: ' . . . the very plan of the family house is anthropomorphic – one end is regarded as the "head" (where males work), the other is the "excretory" end (where the females work). All rubbish must be kept at this end and not round the head, as in the living body!' How many of us male archaeologists would dare to propose such an explanation of rubbish distribution?

Fig. 59 When sherds of pottery or tile, animal bones, nails or other finds not specially categorized as 'small finds' are found, they are put into trays, which are labelled so that their provenance is known and can eventually be recorded, on the objects and on the boxes in which they are stored.

(All photographs in this and the following section by Sidney Renow, except 70a)

Fig. 59

Fig. 60 The excavated pottery, animal bone and finds, other than those which are considered to be important enough to be treated individually as 'small finds', are washed and then dried on racks, keeping the groups together for later analysis.

Fig. 60

Fig. 61 Fig. 61 The sherds of pottery are marked with the site code, the number of the feature or context from which the sherds have come, and the number of the site grid. Marking systems vary from site to site, but most contain enough information to identify the sherd's context if it is sorted into some other combination of finds, say, all the finds from one building, or all the sherds of a particular kind of pottery found on the site.

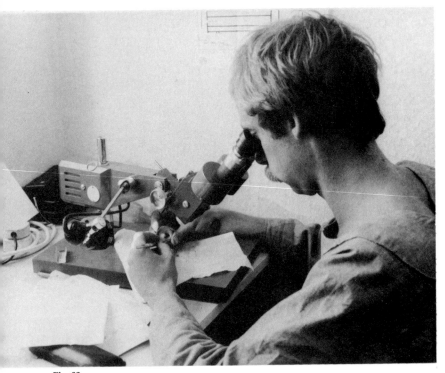

Fig. 62

Fig. 62 *Conservation*
The conservator is cleaning a metal object using a scalpel and binocular microscope.

Fig. 63   *Conservation in the field*
The conservator is here consolidating an object with polyvinyl acetate emulsion before lifting it.

Fig. 63

Fig. 64   *Site photography*
Here the photographer is photographing a find *in situ* with the aid of a tripod which enables him to mount the camera vertically above the object.

Fig. 64

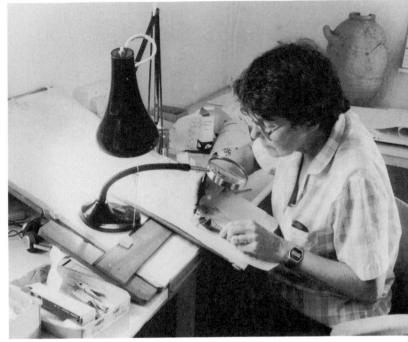

Fig. 65a

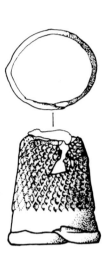

Fig. 65b

Fig. 66

Fig. 65a *Small finds drawing*
The magnifying glass is used to help in drawing the object at twice its actual size. It will be reduced again when it is published. This process makes the drawing of detail much easier.

Fig. 65b A small find drawn in the manner shown in Fig. 65a. It is a silver Roman thimble found at Wroxeter in 1971. It is a remarkable example of the way in which, when an object has reached its most efficient design, it remains unchanged for centuries.
The base diameter of the thimble is 15mm.

Fig. 66 *Dry-sieving*
Dry-sieving recovers many small objects that have escaped the eyes of the trowellers. In one experiment, as much as 10 per cent of all the small finds were recovered from the seive, and an astonishing 50 per cent by weight of pottery, made up mostly of small sherds.

Fig. 67   *Simple wet-sieving*
By washing the spoil that has already
been dry-sieved, even more finds are
recovered, since they can be seen more
easily when they are clean.

Fig. 67

Fig. 68   *Photographing small finds*
The find rests on a sheet of translucent
film and is here lit from 'top-left' which
gives the most 'natural' light and one
which is also used in the drawing of
most small finds. The scale is a
transparent ruler supported a little
above the base, but in the same plane
as the object.

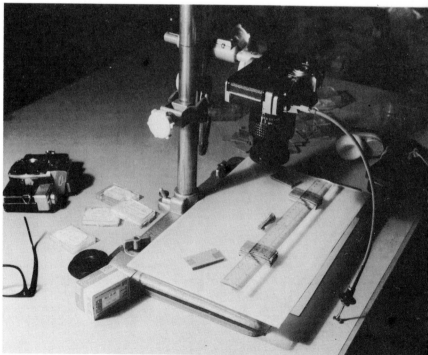

Fig. 68

Fig. 69 *Two finds photographed in the manner shown in Fig. 68*
Fig. 69a A Roman die from Wroxeter. The object has been photographed on a translucent sheet, and placed (with the aid of Blutack) to give the maximum relief, so that three sides can be seen. There is sufficient reflected light for the rings and dots on the shadowed side to be seen clearly.
Fig. 69b A ninth-century AD gilt bronze strap end from Wroxeter. The lighting of the object brings out the low relief of the dragon with interlaced tail and shows the extent of the wear on the surface – this object was quite old when lost, the gilt having been worn off all the surfaces leaving gold only in the crevices and hollows.
The strap end is 45mm long.

Fig. 69a

Fig. 69b

Figs. 70a and **b** A set of toilet implements, made of bone, from the excavations at Dudley Castle, West Midlands. They include an 'ear-spoon' for removing wax, and an implement for shaping the cuticles. The set folded into the decorated bone handle. Such a find might be taken to imply the presence of an aristocratic lady in the castle, if it were not for the fact that an almost identical set was found in the wreck of the *Mary Rose*.

For publication, finds are often drawn as well as photographed, since each method of illustration can be used to highlight or emphasize different features. The drawing is more formal, with sections or profiles, and detail can be made precise; the photograph gives a better sense of the texture of the object and the manner in which it folds.

(Photo: S. Osborne; drawing: S. Lloyd)

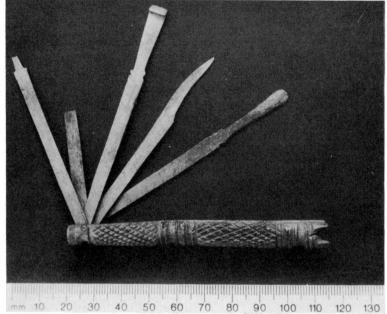

Fig. 70a

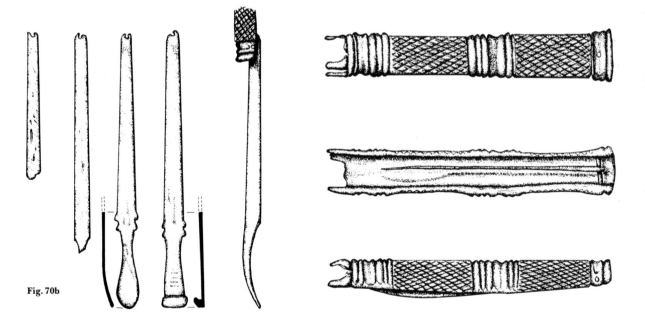

Fig. 70b

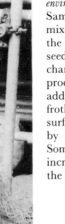

Figs. 71a and **b** *Flotation for environmental evidence*
Samples of soil to be 'floated' are mixed with water and agitated, when the lighter materials, such as charred seeds, fragments of insects or scraps of charcoal float to the surface. This process can sometimes be aided by adding detergent to the water, the froth bringing the fragments to the surface. They can then be recovered by sieving with a fine mesh sieve. Sometimes a nest of sieves with increasingly fine meshes is used to sort the residues.

Fig. 71a

Fig. 71b

Fig. 72

Fig. 72 The site environmentalist examining the results of wet-sieving (the 'flot') under a binocular microscope.

ENVIRONMENTAL EVIDENCE

Human settlements, which are what we principally dig up, do not exist in a vacuum, but are part of what is known as an eco-system – hunting and collecting peoples depend upon the ecological patterns of the edible fauna and flora; farmers are critically dependent on the productivity of the available soils; all are dependent on the fluctuations of climate. The study of the environment in which our sites flourished, or died, has accelerated in recent years, using more and more sophisticated techniques. One of the chief aspects of excavations today is the recovery of environmental evidence of as many kinds as possible, from snails, insects, seeds, charcoals and pollen to animal bones of all kinds, of birds, fish and mammals.

From this evidence it is possible to reconstruct at least something of the natural environment in which the people we are digging up lived, the crops they grew, the animals they bred or hunted or fished, the amount and type of woodland or grassland in the vicinity and patterns of trading in foodstuffs and other commodities. Needless to say, wetland sites or waterlogged pits or wells on dry sites are likely to yield the greatest amount of evidence because of the anaerobic conditions which preserve organic remains.

A waterlogged pit at Hen Domen, Montgomery, produced evidence for no less than 167 plants growing in the vicinity of the site, and 60 types of insect, and this is not exceptional (see Greig, Girling, and Skidmore in Barker and Higham, 1982, pp.59 ff). The synthesis of all the environmental evidence from world-wide excavations and other sources has transformed our understanding of the large-scale fluctuations in plant and animal populations, the clearance of forests and the advent and development of agriculture. On individual excavations, only much narrower inferences can be drawn, but sometimes they are surprising. A small pit containing a mass of animal and fish bones was found close to the foundations of the central tower of Worcester Cathedral. It was surprising to find animal bones there at all, since they seemed to be the remains of a number of meals, with quite high-quality cuts of meat. The most likely explanation for them is that they were the debris from food taken by the masons working on repairs or rebuilding. Among the fish bones were some large vertebrae which we guessed were of salmon from the Severn 100 yards away. However, they were identified by a bone specialist as being of cod. Since Worcester is over 150 miles from the North Sea, the most likely source of cod, it seems certain that the fish was brought across salted, some time in the fifteenth century – a quite unexpected sidelight on the medieval food trade. Such examples could be multiplied from many excavations. They simply show that every scrap of evidence can yield interesting and important information.

CHAPTER SIX

Interpreting the
evidence

PHASING

We have seen that stratification, the superimposition of one layer upon another, provides *relative* dating of events, since if one layer overlies another it must have been placed there later than the one beneath – even if only a few minutes later, as it would be, for example, in the building up of a rampart with successive layers of soil. On the other hand, two superimposed layers may be separated by millennia, where, for instance, a rampart built in prehistoric times has its upper layers shaved off for the construction of a twentieth-century building. (This happened in Worcester, where a Methodist chapel had been built on the remains of a prehistoric rampart, so that, at one point, after the demolition of the chapel, we found a nineteenth-century hymn-book embedded in a layer firmly dated to the Iron Age.)

Needless to say, the building-up or removal of layers are not the only archaeological 'events'. Everything found on an archaeological site is the result of an event of some sort or other, from the building of the foundations of a cathedral to the dropping of a broken brooch. The structural or depositional events (as distinct from the losses of objects) were, in the past, all called *layers*; later, post-holes, pits, ditches, hearths etc. came to be called *features*, as distinct from layers; now the generic term *context* has been adopted for all structural or depositional events. While it is a somewhat abstract noun for describing a concrete floor or the ditch of a hillfort (the OED defines it as 'Parts that precede or follow a passage and fix its meaning') it is ideal for the concept of the stratification diagram or matrix. Such a diagram places every event or context on the site in its correct stratigraphic position relative to all the other contexts on the site. Stratification diagrams have been developed in various ways for some time, but were first formalised by Edward Harris in *Principles of Archaeological Stratigraphy*, London, 1979.

A simple matrix is illustrated in Fig. 73 where a notional section, showing a number of layers with pits cut into them, each numbered sequentially as they were found, is placed into stratigraphic order in the left-hand diagram. The matrix of a whole site is an extension of this principle to embrace every context which is found, and Fig. 84 shows part of the very extensive matrix which has been constructed for the site at Beckford, illustrated in Figs. 26a-d. It will be seen that it is a diagram employing only the context numbers to illustrate and describe their inter-relationship. In the matrix shown, the heavy line outlines a single, very complex structure of ring-ditches, re-cut many times.

In Fig. 75 another part of the same site has been phased on the basis of the inter-relationships of the contexts. For reasons of space, the figure shows only part of the diagram, which is of a stone-floored round house of Iron Age date. It will be appreciated from these examples that the analysis of a large site is a very complex and difficult task, and that the matrix or stratification diagram is a way of demonstrating all the essential relationships in a manner that can be re-assessed at a later date, if required.

The stratification diagram or matrix produces a relative chronology for every event on the site (though, needless to say, there will be a degree of uncertainty about some of them, since their stratigraphic relationship will itself be uncertain). If dates from objects, such as coins, pottery or small finds, or dates derived from scientific examination, such as radio-carbon, thermoluminescence (see the glossary) or tree-ring dating, are inserted into the matrix, then an absolute chronology can be approached. I say, approached, because all of these dates give only a *terminus post* or *ante quem* (for which, see the next section).

ABSOLUTE, OR CHRONOLOGICAL DATING

It is one thing to be reasonably sure of the relative sequences of events on the site; it is quite another to give these events their dates in calendar years. The problem lies in the fact that most absolute dating methods are themselves only relative. For example, it might be thought that a coin, firmly sealed within a rampart, would date the rampart to the date of the coin, at least approximately, on the assumption that one of the workmen building the rampart dropped the coin. But a workman building a motorway might find a Roman coin in a nearby field and lose it the next day while he is helping to build an embankment. No one would make the mistake of dating the motorway to the Roman period, but this is an extreme example. It is much easier to be misled if the date of the coin approximates to the date we expect the rampart or road to belong to.

A moment's reflection will show that the coin, or any other datable artefact, only gives a date either *when* or *after which* the rampart, or road, was constructed. This leads to a general law: a datable object in a layer (or feature, or context) only gives a *terminus post quem*, that is a date *on* or *after which* the layer was deposited. This is perhaps the most important rule in the dating of archaeological sites and one which is often not applied, as it should be, absolutely stringently. The illustrations Figs. 76A-H show variations on this theme. In case you may think that the example in Fig. 76g is rather unlikely, it is worth mentioning that, in the excavations currently being carried out at the bases of the piers of the central tower of the cathedral at Worcester, the foundations of which date, without any doubt at all, to 1084 and the years immediately following, the only pottery found so far in all the layers associated with the earliest building is Roman. Even a large post-hole, presumably for a scaffold pole, had an unabraded Roman sherd in the silt at its bottom. Not only that, but parts of the foundation are packed round with iron slag, almost certainly from the Roman iron foundry known to have been there in the third and fourth centuries, though there is no evidence of later iron smelting in Worcester.

If the cathedral were destroyed to its foundations and dug at some time in the remote future, the excavators would have every excuse for assuming it was a Roman building on the basis of this pottery – unless they remembered the *terminus post quem* rule.

The other rule which is of paramount importance is the *terminus ante quem* rule, which states that if the date of a layer or feature is known, then all the layers or features which underly it or which it cuts must be earlier. This rule is also best described with the aid of illustrations, see Figs. 76H, 77a and 77b.

INTERPRETATION

It is one thing to excavate a site and record all its layers, its features and the finds contained in them; it is quite another to understand what they mean, to determine the way in which each deposit was formed and its significance in the development of the site, and then to put it all together into a coherent sequence of events. A description of a layer, however detailed, does not explain how it got there nor why, but it is important to keep the observed evidence, so far as possible, separate from its interpretation. This is often very difficult. Sites are not dug (yet) by automatons, and it is impossible to stop interpretations floating into the mind even while the evidence is appearing. To give a simple example – a strip of packed pebbles leading to a gap in a wall suggests 'path' long before it has even been properly cleaned. It may prove, later, to be something quite different. It is very important, therefore, to keep as open a mind as possible, and to be prepared always to change first thoughts, or even second thoughts, in the light of further, incompatible, evidence. Some excavators advocate strongly that interpretation should be avoided until the excavation is complete, in order to avoid subjective thinking, or the danger of finding what you want to find, of making

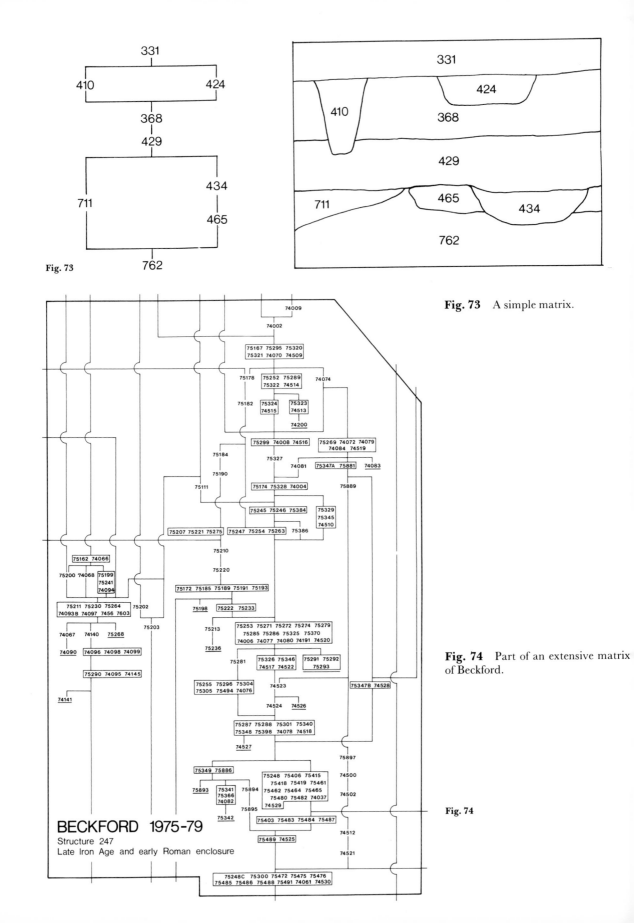

Fig. 73 A simple matrix.

Fig. 74 Part of an extensive matrix of Beckford.

BECKFORD 1975-79
Structure 247
Late Iron Age and early Roman enclosure

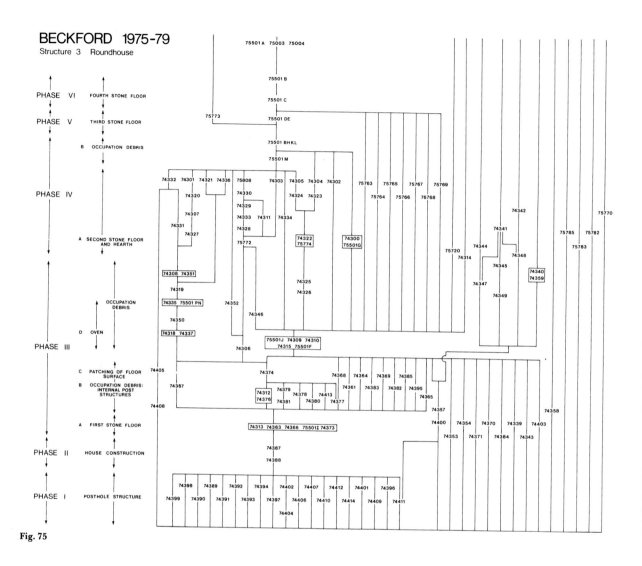

Fig. 75 Phasing of Beckford on the basis of the inter-relationships of the context.

Fig. 76 *Terminus post quem*

A A clay floor is bounded by post-holes. The floor contains three coins of the second century AD. Coin D is of the first century. The floor was therefore laid *during or after* the second century AD.

On the basis of this evidence alone, the floor could be twentieth-century. It certainly might be fifth-century or Anglo-Saxon. However, if coin D was third-century, coins A, B, and C are all negated as dating evidence, and the floor which seals coin D must be third-century or later.

B Coin D is first-century AD; coin C second-century; coin B third-century and coin A fourth-century. Here is a fairly common situation, somewhat simplified, in which we have a superficially plausible sequence of dating evidence which suggests that the four layers span the whole Roman period in sequence. However, if we apply the *terminus post quem* rule strictly, as we must, the whole lot could be post Roman, even modern. Other dating factors would have to be discovered and assessed before a Roman sequence could be maintained.

C In this figure there is increased probability that the layers above A were laid down in the second – third century and the third – fourth century *but no certainty*. Again A is crucial. If it is a ninth-century coin or thirteenth-century pot, all of the material above it must be considered residual.

D In this similarly plausible sequence, if A is an otherwise undatable sherd or object one must be careful not to use a false *terminus ante quem* reasoning and maintain that A must be earlier than first – second-century. It may ultimately prove to be, say, fourth-century, when the two layers above take their *terminus post quem* from it.

E The two objects A and B, though found together in a pit, tell us *nothing* about each other except that they were buried in the pit together at some time *at or later than* the date of the later of the two objects. However, if object C can be shown to be of later date than either A or B then the whole sequence takes its *terminus post quem* from C.

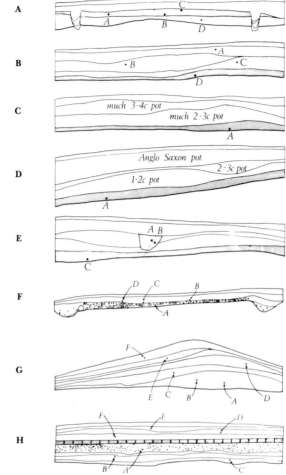

Fig. 76

F A is a Roman coin or sherd, B is a medieval spur.

It is tempting to see this as a Roman road still in use in medieval times. However, the road could be of any date, from the Roman period onward. (It cannot be prehistoric if the sherd is thoroughly sealed.) It is even possible that the spur was an antique dropped recently.

G This illustration is based on an actual example (at Quatford in Shropshire, Mason and Barker, 1961).

    F – 19th-century sherd
    E – medieval sherd
    D – medieval bronze object
    C – Roman sherd
    B – neolithic flint
    A – 1881 halfpenny

The presumed medieval rampart was shown to be dated to 1881 or later by the presence of the Victorian halfpenny.

The danger here is that the halfpenny might not have been dropped, or that it would not have been found if the cutting had been made elsewhere along the 'rampart'. In fact, the bank was formed by ploughing during the 1939-45 war, so that the 1881 coin gives a *terminus post quem* some 60 years too early.

H All the layers under the tiled floor including finds A, B and C in the illustration are given a *terminus ante quem* by the floor. If the floor is made of, say, fourteenth-century tiles then all the layers beneath must be fourteenth-century or earlier. They might be prehistoric. Be sure that the floor has not been taken up and relaid in later times, perhaps in a nineteenth-century restoration.

A clear example of the *terminus ante quem* argument can be seen in **Figs. 77a** and **b**. A small excavation was recently carried out under the floor of the splendid crypt of Worcester Cathedral, begun by Bishop Wulstan in 1084. The floor itself rested on loose earth and small rubble which lay over a concrete raft, A, some six inches below the floor. The free-standing columns were founded not on the concrete raft, but on large fragments of rubble used to pack them to reach the desired floor level. Among these lumps of rubble was a fragment of carved stone (B, and Fig. 77b). Its position under the column provides it with a firm *terminus ante quem* of 1084; in other words, since the rubble packing is earlier than the column, whose date is known, the carving must also be earlier than the column, i.e. 1084. In fact the carving is typical of Anglo-Saxon sculpture of the ninth or tenth centuries. Furthermore, the concrete raft, by the same argument, must itself also be earlier than 1084. Since it appears not to be of the same build as the columns (since, unless the masons had made a gross error in laying out, the columns would hardly have needed to be packed with rubble), it seems to belong to an earlier building, perhaps the crypt of one of the Anglo-Saxon minsters which are known to have preceded the Norman cathedral. Paradoxically, the same example can be used to illustrate the *terminus post quem* argument. If one imagines that the cathedral had long ago been destroyed, and was being excavated without prior knowledge of what it was, the fragment of sculpture would give a *terminus post quem* to the column base. If the date of the sculpture was known on general grounds, it would be clear that the column base must be later than the ninth – tenth centuries – in other words, it could *not* be Roman, but it could be medieval, or of any date between the late Saxon period and the present day.

Fig. 77a

Fig. 77b

Fig. 78

Fig. 78 If only all dating were as easy . . . This is one of several mid-eighteenth-century burials excavated from the churchyard of St Mary's, Ware, Herts. Very fragmentary remains of a wooden coffin still retained the brass studs which had been used to spell out the initials, age and year of death of the deceased. Careful excavation with dental picks and small paint brushes was necessary to reveal the full detail of these very precise pieces of dating evidence. (Photo: courtesy of Clive Partridge, Director of the Hart Archaeological Trust)

serious mistakes because the interpretation is, inevitably, not based on a full consideration of all the evidence, which will not be available until much post-excavation work has been done. This austere view has much to commend it (though it could make site tours rather arid, and would certainly not satisfy news reporters' demands for instant interpretation), and it is important to keep the objectively observed evidence separated from the interpretation, so far as this is possible. I think, though, that our inevitable tendency to interpret as we go along can be turned to good advantage. Every excavation begins by asking questions, however broad, of the site. As the excavation proceeds and the evidence emerges, so the questions change, or entirely new ones arise. This can only happen if there is a degree of interpretation in the thinking which goes on all the time. The important thing is to be continually aware of the difference between the evidence and its interpretation, so that it becomes possible to discard completely an interpretation which does not fit the emerging evidence. This requires a degree of 'lateral' thinking, the ability to clear the mind of one interpretation and substitute another, or more than one, which may fit the evidence better. Sometimes, in fact, it may be impossible to decide between two or more interpretations, either because there simply is not enough evidence or because what there is is ambiguous. In such cases, the alternatives should be published, with their supporting arguments, so that the reader is not faced with a take-it-or-leave-it conclusion, but has the chance to make up his own mind.

It is not possible to describe all the problems of interpretation which will occur on a complex excavation, but I believe that excavators should attempt to explain, as a first step, the origins and the purpose of each layer and feature they find. In many cases, the answers will be obvious, but there will be many more where they are not. For instance, it may be crucial to decide whether or not a layer of grey, silty earth within a building has been deposited naturally or not, since on this decision will rest the interpretation of whether it is, say, a beaten earth floor or, alternatively, the result of a flood. Not every hole in the ground held a post, nor is every pebble spread a floor, so that it is essential to look very critically at the derivation and function of all the features that have been recorded before putting them together to make structures. Figs. 81a-d show the result of a critical look at one small part of the site of the basilica at Wroxeter.

A number of other drawings and photographs in this book illustrate aspects of interpretation, particularly Figs. 79a, 79b; 80; 83a and 83b, and I hope that the texts which accompany them throw some light on what is, in the end, the essence of our work. A further example, using both positive and negative evidence, may be illuminating.

The excavation of the motte and bailey castle at Hen Domen, Montgomery, and particularly the interpretation of the excavated evidence, has been profoundly influenced by presuppositions based on all that we know, or think we know, about the period following the

Norman Conquest, and in particular its defensive structures. The site was chosen for excavation because of its fine earthworks of motte and bailey type (Figs. 29a, 87) on the assumption that they were those of an early timber castle, and, further, that they were those of the castle built by Roger de Montgomery between *c.*AD 1070 and 1086, which is mentioned by name among the Domesday entries for Shropshire.

Roger de Montgomery was one of William the Conqueror's greatest magnates and the castle was sufficiently important to him to be named by him nostalgically after his birthplace in the Calvados region of Normandy. On the fall of Robert de Belleme, one of Roger's sons, and the demise of the Earldom of Shropshire in 1102, the castle passed to a lesser family, that of the de Boulers.

Since the beginning of the excavation, therefore, our understanding of everything found, from the plans of buildings to pottery, from arrowheads to horseshoe nails, has been coloured by the knowledge that this was an aristocratic site of crucial strategic importance in this part of the Welsh border, since it is situated close to a major ford over the River Severn.

But there have been, even after twenty-three seasons of intensive excavation, no finds which could dispassionately be called 'aristocratic', nothing, apart from the defences themselves, to suggest that the site was occupied by a succession of wealthy and powerful families.

It therefore occurred to the writer, to wonder how, if we could clear our minds of all preconceptions, we would interpret Hen Domen? What conclusions would we draw about the people who lived here if we knew nothing of medieval life? What, in fact, distinguishes it from a small prehistoric defended site?

The presence of the motte prevents the earthworks from looking prehistoric, but there are a number of ring-works (see the glossary) in the region which cannot, by inspection, be dated more closely than within a bracket which includes the later Bronze Age at one end and the later thirteenth century at the other, and, if one stands with one's back to the motte (as in Fig. 53a), the bailey at Hen Domen could well be one of these.

The evidence of the structures revealed by the excavation (Fig. 88) is very varied but none of it is different in kind from the methods of timber building used in the previous thousand or more years. There is nothing here which could not have been fashioned at least from Roman times onwards – there are no suggestions of the highly elaborate joints of only slightly later date found in medieval barns and church roofs.

All the constructional methods, using post-holes and wattle walls, or clay walls strengthened with small irregularly-spaced posts, are undatable in style, as were perhaps the buildings they represent. The writer always intended, when reconstructing the Hen Domen buildings, to have them bristling with dragons at the corners, like the motte towers on the Bayeux Tapestry, or the stave churches of Norway, or the church at Kilpeck, only 50 miles away. But though a good deal of waterlogged worked timber has been found on the site, none of it has any decorative carving, even of the simplest – all is utilitarian. Nor have any of the pieces of leather found been tooled or punched decoratively. In fact, the earliest levels on the site, those datable to before *c.*1125, yield almost no finds at all. There are tiny scraps of pottery derived from pots thought to have been imported from elsewhere, probably the Midlands. The only finds of metal are nails, knives, arrowheads and other less identifiable objects. The finds are, in fact, little different in quality or quantity from those found at a small defended Iron Age site of the tribe of the Cornovii near Shrewsbury, dug by the writer and others in 1965 (forthcoming). And the Cornovii have been described as 'a poor, backward rural community'. We seem to be getting close to Sir Mortimer Wheeler's description of William the Conqueror as a 'scratch-mark-ware chieftain'.

Is this fair? Did Roger's men and Baldwyn de Bouler's family live like Iron Age peasants? Or was the Iron Age site itself the home of a Cornovian aristocratic family? Their round houses were certainly bigger than any building yet found at Hen Domen, even if not so substantially founded.

The contrast with the Roman sites of the area is startling. At Wroxeter the quantities of pottery and small finds of all kinds are enormous – over 100,000 sherds of pottery have been recovered, from the upper layers only, of an area approximately 140 by 30 metres; the annual yield of coins is about 250 and there are hundreds of brooches, hairpins and beads, together with all kinds of decorative metalwork, carved objects of bone, shale and jet. There is also much evidence of trade with the Continent and as far away as the eastern Mediterranean. The object traded furthest to Hen Domen seems to be a jug from the Stamford area of Lincolnshire. Nothing even from Normandy can be identified.

Yet both Wroxeter and Hen Domen lack one vital strand which we know was of the greatest significance in the lives of their inhabitants – at neither site is there any evidence of Christianity. If we knew nothing of Romano-British or Anglo-Norman culture we should have no inkling from these sites of that all-pervading influence. Yet there is every reason to believe that there was a Bishop of Wroxeter from the fourth century onwards, that is, the period under excavation there, and the Normans were devout fighters who did penance for the souls of those they killed.

If so powerful a force as Christianity cannot easily be detected, other aspects of the spiritual and intellectual life of the site will be equally elusive. We may guess from the deer and wild boar bones on the site that Baldwyn and his entourage enjoyed hunting, but we do not know their taste in poetry and music – if any. And though we can assume from what we know of castle life in general that Baldwyn's wife and children lived with him, there is little, if anything, among the finds to suggest the presence of women, and nothing, such as toys or feeding bottles (known

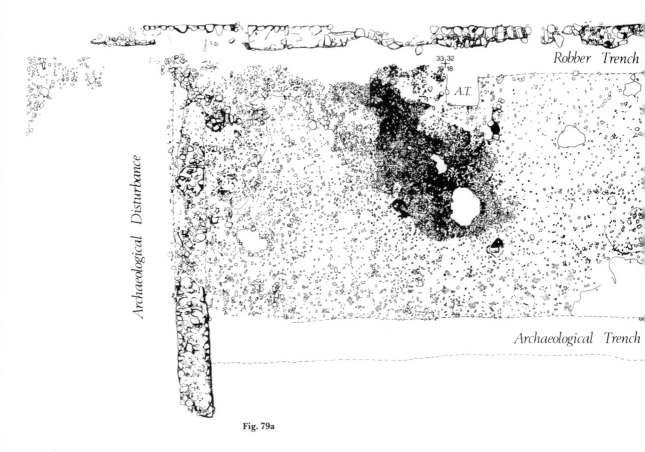

Archaeological Disturbance

33,32
19 18

A.T.

Robber Trench

Archaeological Trench

Fig. 79a

Figs. 79a and **b** are two drawings of a building from the excavation of the Baths Basilica at Wroxeter. **Fig. 79a** is a redrawing of the evidence as it was recorded in the field. Though originally drawn in colour, it has had to be redrawn in black and white because colour printing is prohibitively expensive. The drawing includes all the evidence as seen. **Fig. 79b** extracts from this drawing what we believe to be significant structurally, and attempts to interpret it. The next stage, which we have not yet reached, will be to try to envisage and draw the building in three dimensions. Needless to say, the further we go upwards, away from the evidence on the ground, the less certain the reconstruction will be, so that the roof covering will be almost complete conjecture – though not quite, since, as there was no trace of roof tiles or slates, it is very probable that the roof covering was of thatch or shingles, an example of the value of negative evidence.

The building is sited in the north-eastern corner of the precinct of the baths and it is bounded on the north by a wall which we believe to have been standing during the life of the building. The evidence consists of eight post-holes and a number of pebble spreads, shown in **Fig. 79a**. In **Fig. 79b** the presumed wall-lines have been indicated, together with the suggested positions of the doors, which were approached by the pebble spreads, presumed to be paths. A gap in the wall-line on the northern side is presumed to mark another entrance, this time into the portico of the baths insula. It will be seen that **Fig. 79a** the pebble spreads appear to have straight boundaries; these perhaps mark the positions of partitions, shown with a dotted line on **Fig. 79b**. It is presumed that the building leant-to against the northern wall, though any evidence there may have been has been lost in a robber trench and in two small earlier archaeological trenches marked AT.

The building is thought to have been a barn or storeroom, as was its successor (see Barker, 1982, 234-237). In these two drawings the evidence as recorded in the field has been kept separate from the suggested interpretation, so that the reader is not presented simply with a *fait accompli*, but can make up his/her own mind.

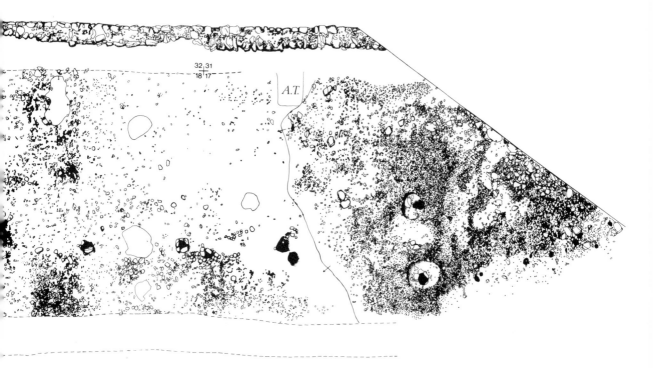

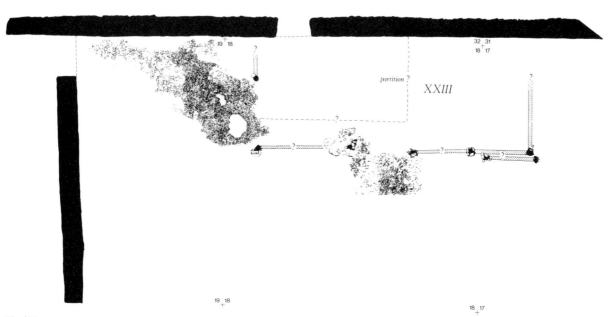

Fig. 79b

Fig. 80

Fig. 81a

Fig. 80 is of the worn entrance threshold of the Baths Basilica at Wroxeter looking out into the western portico. The low-level photograph shows how the threshold, and therefore the door, or at least the opening where the door had been, was still in use long after the portico had lost its original surface and been covered with pebbles and larger stones, which are clearly worn by the passage of feet out along a roughly laid path.

Figs. 81a, b, c and **d** show the remains of the foundation (*stylobate*) of the portico colonnade of the Baths Basilica at Wroxeter. The pecked areas W1 and W2 are the positions of the column bases; from these the distance between the columns down the whole length of the portico can be determined. However, the photographs also show very interesting patterns of wear on the surfaces of the stones. While it would be expected that there would be wear between the columns, the stone at X shows wear along the edge and over the pecking which strongly suggests that there was a lot of traffic *after* the columns had gone, implying continuing occupation of the site (on a considerable scale, since the stones are very hard) after the destruction of the public buildings of which the portico formed a part.

In addition, the two stones at Y and Z are heavily worn on each side of the gap between them, suggesting that there was here a path or passage across the portico, not necessarily, though probably, after the columns had gone. (Photos: author)

Fig. 81b

Fig. 81c

Fig. 81d

Fig. 82 This photograph of one of the mortar floors of the Baths Basilica at Wroxeter shows what appears to be the line of partition dividing off part of the north aisle. The partition was almost certainly of wood, which was later replaced, on a slightly different alignment, by a rough stone wall. The photograph was taken in the early morning (the arrow points to north) in order to show the slight indentation by glancing light.
(Photo: author)

Fig. 82

Figs. 83a and **b** These photographs, of the northern portico of the Baths Basilica at Wroxeter, show how some ephemeral evidence is revealed only when a large area is meticulously cleared. The ranging rods are laid along the lines of joists which held a boardwalk running the length of the portico. The faint traces of the joists are due to their weight (and the weight of the people who walked on the boards above) compressing the underlying layers. Subsequently the trowellers sensed the harder material and left it, removing the softer material on either side (**Fig. 83b**) to reveal the long parallel lines.

Fig. 83 ▶

Fig. 83b

Fig. 84

Fig. 84 A zig-zag shaped feature on the edge of the motte at Hastings (thought to be the motte of William the Conqueror's first castle in England) was sectioned and, surprisingly, proved to be a Second World War trench, revetted with sandbags. The bags were rotted away leaving only their fillings, which can be seen on each side of the section. They were dated by a beer bottle top. (Photo: author)

Fig. 85a

Fig. 85b

Fig. 85a During the course of excavations in Northampton in 1974 and again in 1980, five Saxon mortar mixers were found close to St Peter's Church. The mixers, circular bowls cut down into the ground or built on its surface, varied in diameter between 2 and 3 metres and all contained residues from mixing, which facilitated the interpretation of these initially enigmatic structures. All had evidence of a central post and several had traces of basket-work round their perimeter. Mixer 3 had a central ridge in which further holes were visible. On removal of the top residue from the mixer, striations could be seen in the underlying mix, which lined up with the ridge holes. These striations were almost certainly the grooves scored by rotating paddles. Presumably the earlier residue was still soft when a fresh mix was being prepared and different consistencies of the respective mixes preserved the indications of the rotary action of the mixer. Traces of grooves evidencing rotary motion were also present in the mixers excavated in 1980.

The scale is 1 metre long.

Fig. 85b On the basis of the evidence shown in **Fig. 85a**, this reconstruction drawing has been made.

(Photo and drawing: courtesy of John Williams)

WROXETER · BATHS BASILICA · Distribution of Wall Plaster

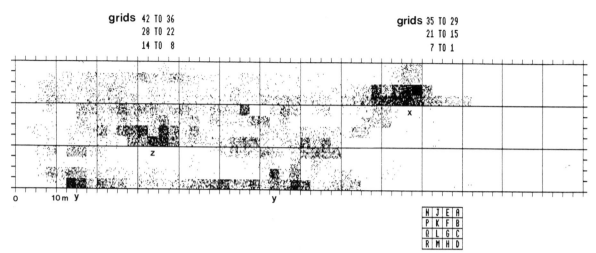

grids 42 TO 36   **grids** 35 TO 29
28 TO 22   21 TO 15
14 TO 8   7 TO 1

Fig. 86

Fig. 86 This is a computer plot of the distribution of wall plaster found in the excavation of the Baths Basilica at Wroxeter. The find spots of the wall plaster were recorded in 2½ metre squares and this is how they have been plotted. The significance of the distribution has not yet been studied, though the concentrations at x and y can be accounted for, in part, by the fact that they are close to walls which still stand to a height of a metre or so. The concentration at z is not so easily explained, and must almost certainly have been brought on to the site from elsewhere. Such a plot is only the starting point for the study of the wall plaster distribution, and goes hand in hand with a study of the painted patterns on the plaster, and reconstruction of those patterns. (Plot: Georgina Shaw)

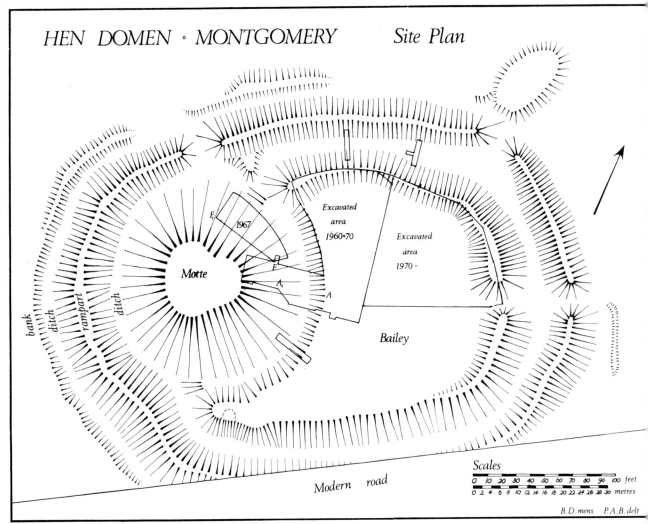

Fig. 87

Fig. 87   Plan of the motte and bailey castle at Hen Domen, Montgomery and the excavated area shown in Fig. 88.

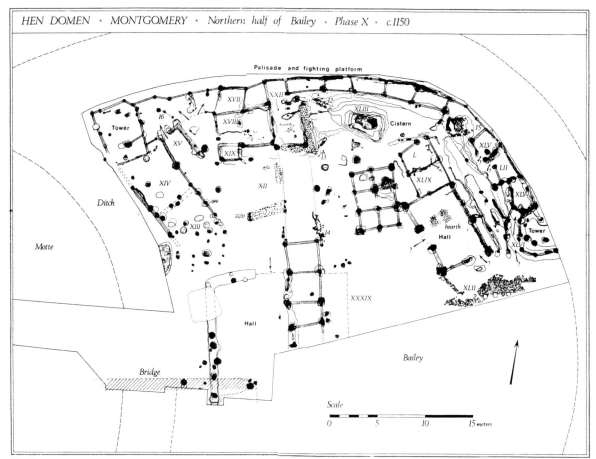

Fig. 88

elsewhere in pottery), to suggest children. It is probable that Roger's first castle was a garrison entirely manned by soldiers and that from 1102 onward the castle became residential, but there is at present no *archaeological* evidence to support this assumption.

While accepting, however, that there are many limitations of archaeological evidence, we must look for positive conclusions that can be drawn about the site in its earlier years and the people who lived there.

Everything points to a life of great simplicity, shorn of extraneous trappings and ornament. The bailey is at all times crowded with buildings, but only two have any sign of heating (though the use of braziers, perhaps even in upper rooms, and therefore not archaeologically discernible, cannot be discounted). The impression one gets is of a life of great hardiness, lived mainly out of doors, except in the worst weather and at night – not unlike all-year-round camping. There is nothing to suggest literacy among any of the castle inhabitants; they clearly used very little coin (only one coin has been found in 23 years of excavation); they ate, as one would expect, beef, mutton and pork and some deer (though there is less antler, worked or unworked, than one would expect); there is very little bread wheat and no sign of any cultivated fruits, such as plum or apple (though there are some wild blackberries) and no imported delicacies such as figs or grapes. The picture is, in fact, very close to that of the hard simple life, with few social graces, spent chiefly in the open, that one would deduce from the excavation of prehistoric sites here or elsewhere on the Welsh border.

By the early thirteenth century all that had changed. The new stone castle at Montgomery was decorated with stiff-leaf capitals as fine as those at the cathedrals of Westminster, Wells or Lincoln, and with elegant mouldings for the glazed windows, and it is reasonable to assume that the rest of the castle was in keeping. Even allowing for the fact that New Montgomery Castle was a royal foundation, and that the de Boulers were, by comparison, poor, nevertheless, Hen Domen is the site of their only castle and one might expect what movable wealth they had to be concentrated there. It had been suggested that the de Boulers and similar families might have had their wealth tied up in livestock rather than in finery – if so, the comparison with prehistoric peoples is even closer. At Hen Domen, and particularly in the earlier decades, we seem to be in a quite different world from that of the courtly aristocratic life commonly envisaged in the medieval castle.

CHAPTER SEVEN

The publication of excavations

Until comparatively recently, archaeological publication tended to take two quite distinct forms: on the one hand, the academic report in a specialist journal or monograph, and on the other, the popularizing book, called something like *Great Archaeological Discoveries of the World* or *The Testimony of the Spade*. The increasing size and complexity of modern excavations has modified both these sorts of publication. The totality of the evidence from large, even medium sized, excavations cannot now be contained within one or two volumes of reasonable size, and, even where it is, the expense of printing the comparatively small numbers of such volumes which the publishers can hope to sell puts them beyond the reach of students, the public in general and even most professionals, and so they are confined to libraries.

In addition to the problem of expense, it is now quite impossible even for specialists to read all that is published in their fields – the volume of printed material of all kinds is overwhelming. This means, of course, that specialists are tempted to specialize more and more narrowly in order to keep up with the flow of information, or, more probably, to rely on short reports or abstracts. Such condensation suffers, of course, from many of the deficiencies of one-page summaries of the plays of Shakespeare – distortions are inevitable, subtleties are lost, and all that is left is a bare outline, a silhouette.

The solution may lie in what now appears to be developing – a series of publications graded in size and complexity. *Leaflets* may be handed out while the excavation is in progress, followed by more substantial *interim reports* which, while essentially ephemeral, keep the public and other archaeologists informed of progress, and eventually form a very interesting record of the development of the excavation and the changing interpretations of the excavators. Popular, but substantial, *reports*, may also be produced, their size depending on the size and importance of the excavation; at their best these are highly readable and at the same time reliable (and are, it has been remarked with a degree of cynicism, the only ones most archaeologists will buy . . .). Among the best of these are Leslie Alcock's *By South Cadbury is that Camelot*, Thames and Hudson, 1972; Richard Hall's *York, The Viking Dig*, and *Danebury, Anatomy of an Iron Age Hillfort*, Batsford, 1983, by Barry Cunliffe, all of which should be considered required reading by readers of this book.

Next in order of completeness are the *academic publications* of excavations, as volumes of journals, or as monographs. In order to cut down on the book size, the addition of microfiche is now common, usually in a pocket at the back. Microfiche consists of a sheet of film approximately 15cm by 10cm printed with approximately 60 negatives of text, or positives of colour slides, for example. While these save space (though not, it is now claimed, money), their shortcomings are that they have to be read with a machine and that without two machines it is difficult to compare plans or drawings. There is a limit to the size of the normal screen, so that very large drawings will not easily reduce sufficiently to be put on microfiche. It is claimed by its proponents that soon every home will have a microfiche reader, but this is doubted by many. It also has the drawback that it is not easy to use a microfiche reader in the bath or in bed, where many excavators do their research . . .

Finally there is the whole *excavation archive*, together with all the finds thought worthy of preservation, brought up to a standard of presentation suitable for consultation, curated in a publicly accessible place, such as a museum, or record office, or the offices of an archaeological body, such as a Trust. This is then available for those, who will only ever be few, who need to study the whole operation, either to attempt its reinterpretation at some future date, or who may be proposing to excavate on the same or an adjacent site. Would that those who have dug at Wroxeter over the last 100 years had left a similar archive . . .

Excavation reports recommended for further reading will be found marked with an asterisk in the bibliography.

EXCAVATION AND THE PUBLIC

Until recently, excavations were either private, being carried out by amateurs from Pitt-Rivers and Schliemann onward, or were funded by museums (anxious for the finds) or universities. It is only within the last fifteen to twenty years that, chiefly in response to the realisation of the extent of destruction of archaeological sites of all kinds, a great deal of public money has been put into excavation. This is not the place, however, in which to chronicle the rise of rescue archaeology; this has been done by Philip Rahtz in *Rescue Archaeology*, Penguin, 1974, and by Barri Jones in *Past Imperfect: the story of rescue archaeology*, 1984. Now, government agencies, such as the Historic Buildings and Monuments Commission, together with the Manpower Services Commission, many Statutory Authorities, such as the Gas Board and the Coal Board and

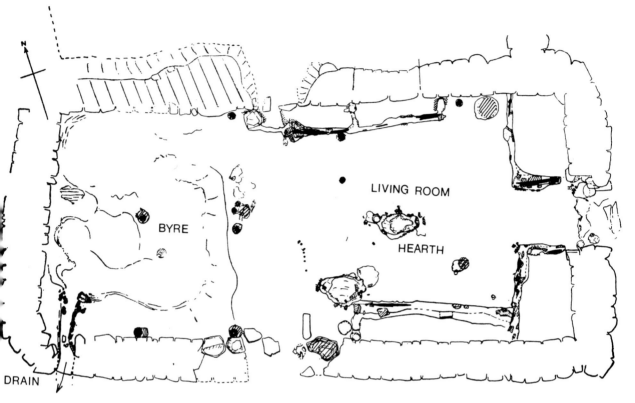

Fig. 89a   Mawgan Porth Cornwall. Comprehensive field plan of the long room in the upper courtyard-house (features of phases 1 and 2 not distinguished). The byre is to the left, the living-room to the right. Length of room internally, 33 feet.

Fig. 89a-e   One of the principal ways in which archaeological sites are brought to life for the general public is by 'reconstruction drawings', and the supreme exponent of this art was the late Alan Sorrell. This drawing, **Fig. 89a**, is of a peasant long-house at Mawgan Porth, in Cornwall, excavated by Rupert Bruce-Mitford between 1950 and 1954. The site consisted of two groups of small houses set around courtyards. They had clay-bonded walls of roughly coursed stone with roofs of turf and branches supported on timber uprights with poles to form the roof frame. The eastern end of the building illustrated had a hearth in its centre and was furnished with box beds made by setting slate slabs into slots cut into the floor (see **Fig. 89b**); the other end of the house had a drain set in one corner and post settings for a partition – it was clearly for cattle, which could thereby be kept in warmth and safety, especially during the winter. This is a house type which, in varying forms, is common all over Europe in the medieval period – most deserted medieval villages in England which have been excavated contain houses of this type.

Fig. 89b

Fig. 89c

Fig. 89d

Fig. 89e

Figs. 89c, d and **e** are of a small barn at Blakemoor Gate in Shropshire (see also Figs. 4a-e). Although it does not contain living quarters, it is very like the house at Mawgan Porth in its construction and in the partitions at the far end seen in **Fig. 89d** and **e**. It was in use until the 1950s. If, when it has completely disappeared above ground, it is excavated, the evidence will be extraordinarily like that of the building of 900 years earlier at Mawgan Porth.
(Plan: by kind permission of Rupert Bruce-Mitford; photos: author)

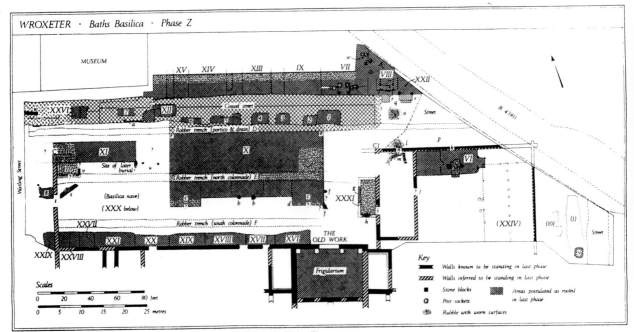

Fig. 90a *Wroxeter:* plan of the latest occupation on the site of the baths-basilica.

Fig. 90b is an attempt to show what the buildings of the final occupation of the city centre at Wroxeter may have looked like. The drawing is based on what might be considered the flimsiest of evidence – platforms of rubble laid horizontally over the remains of the basilica (**Fig. 90a**). There are, however, convincing reasons to believe that the platforms were deliberately laid, and that the plan of the largest building, in the centre of the picture, was symmetrical about two large fragments of masonry, which had been placed as foundations for the columns of a portico. Elsewhere also there was evidence of symmetrical facades of buildings constructed along one of the east-west streets (Barker, 1980). This drawing is a first attempt –

there is little doubt that, in the light of further analysis of the evidence and discussion with architectural historians, it will be extensively modified. For example, it is probably too wide for its height and the evidence for the 'wings' is uncertain, and they could be thrust further forward.

One problem which arises from the publication of such a drawing is that it is seized on by authors who want to illustrate their books on late Roman Britain, often without the very strong reservations which ought to accompany a piece of kite-flying like this. This is, of course, the danger with all interim reports: that they will be used as if they were final, instead of accounts of work in progress.

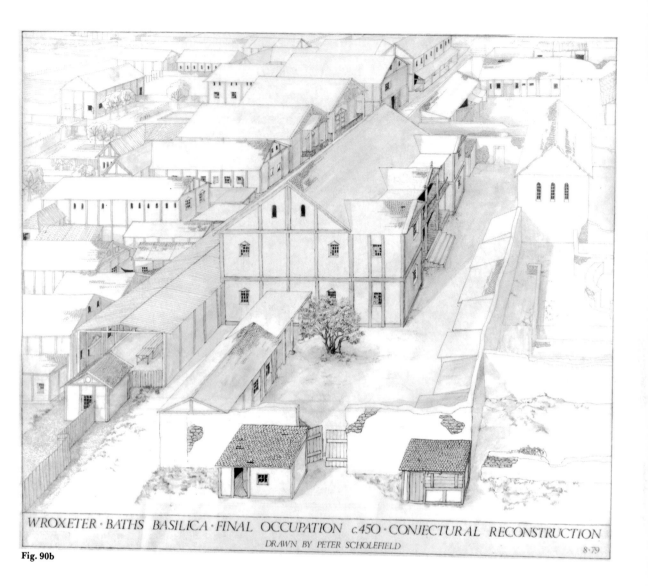

WROXETER · BATHS BASILICA · FINAL OCCUPATION c.450 · CONJECTURAL RECONSTRUCTION

DRAWN BY PETER SCHOLEFIELD

8·79

Fig. 90b

Fig. 91a

Figs. 91a-f In 1971 Philip Rahtz and Ken Sheriden excavated the remains of a Saxon water mill at Tamworth in Staffordshire. **Fig. 91a** is a photograph of the timber foundations of the mill, preserved in the waterlogged condition of the soil. Radio-carbon dates from these timbers all lie within the eighth century, in the time of Mercian pre-eminence, when there is evidence, in the form of royal charters signed by King Offa, which suggests that there was a palace here, served very probably by the mill discovered in 1971.

Fig. 91b is a diagramatic plan of the mill with its chute, by-pass and wheel restored, and **Fig. 91c** is a section through the mill, in a reconstruction based firmly on the evidence revealed by the excavation. The mill is of the horizontal, or Norse, type (as distinct from the now more familiar vertical type which is much more powerful).

Fig. 91d shows Mr F.W.B. Charles' proposed full-scale reconstruction of the mill; and the two photographs, **Figs. 91e** and **91f** are of Mr Charles' model made in advance of the full-scale reconstruction.

(Drawings: courtesy of Philip Rahtz and Freddie Charles; photos: courtesy of Martin Charles)

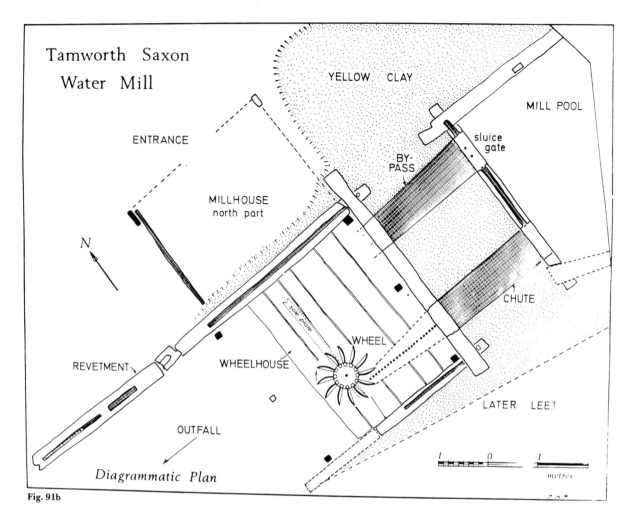

Tamworth Saxon
Water Mill

YELLOW CLAY

MILL POOL

ENTRANCE

sluice gate

BY-PASS

MILLHOUSE
north part

N

CHUTE

sole plate

WHEEL

REVETMENT

WHEELHOUSE

LATER LEET

OUTFALL

Diagrammatic Plan

Fig. 91b

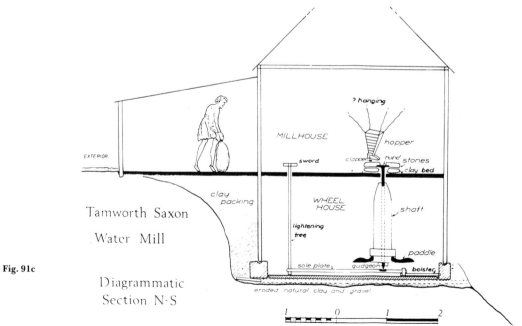

? hanging

MILLHOUSE

hopper

EXTERIOR

sword

clapper   runner stones

clay bed

clay packing

Tamworth Saxon

WHEEL HOUSE

shaft

Water Mill

lightening tree

paddle

Fig. 91c

sole plate   gudgeon   boister

Diagrammatic
Section N-S

eroded natural clay and gravel

metres

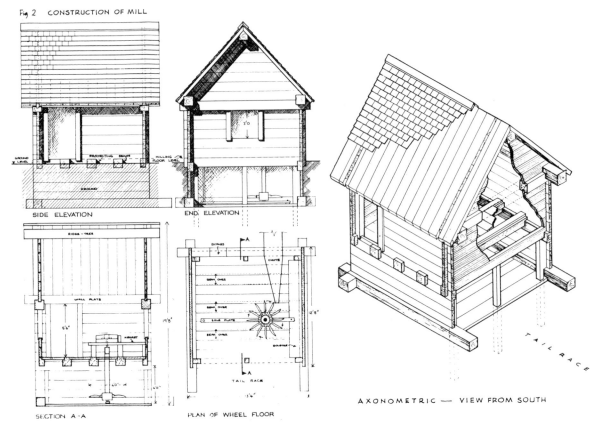

Fig 2 CONSTRUCTION OF MILL
PROJECTING BEAMS
MILLING FLOOR LEVEL
GROUND LEVEL
GROUND
3'0
SIDE ELEVATION
END ELEVATION
RIDGE - TREE
WALL PLATE
5'6"
19'8"
4'0"
BYPASS
A
CHUTE
BEAM OVER
SOLE PLATE
BOLSTER
12'8"
TAIL RACE
15'4"
SECTION A-A
PLAN OF WHEEL FLOOR
TAIL RACE
AXONOMETRIC — VIEW FROM SOUTH

Fig. 91d

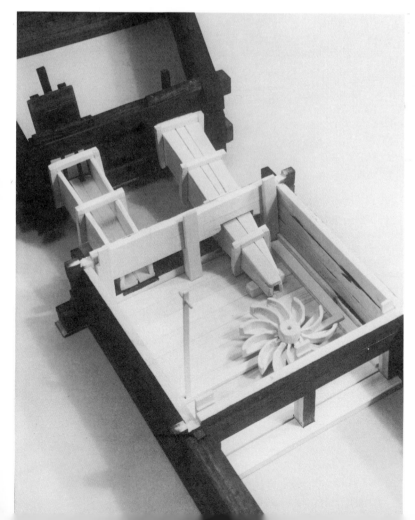

Fig. 92

Fig. 92 is an impression of the entrance to the forum at Wroxeter Roman city about AD 130, painted by A. Forestier in 1925. It is inaccurate in many details, but it is 'truthful' in that it provides a vivid evocation of what life may well have been like in a provincial Roman town. It should be compared with the impression by Alan Sorrell of life in a house at Mawgan Porth (Fig. 89b); with the provisional reconstruction of the building at the centre of Wroxeter 300 years later (Fig. 90b), and with the drawings and model of the Tamworth water mill (Figs. 91a-f).

Fig. 93

Fig. 93 *Excavation and the public*
One of the obligations on archaeologists, and especially on those who are using public money for excavations, is to tell the public why and how their money is being used. Here, on an open day at Wroxeter, a supervisor is explaining the site to one of many groups of visitors. They will then be invited to visit an exhibition which shows the results of the work in plans and photographs together with notable finds.
(Photo: Sidney Renow)

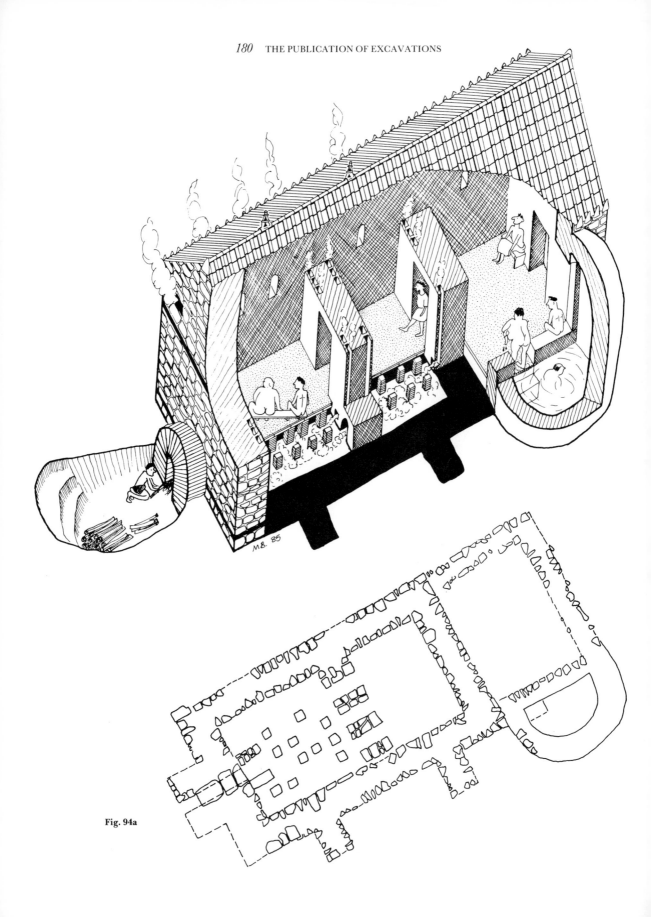

Fig. 94a

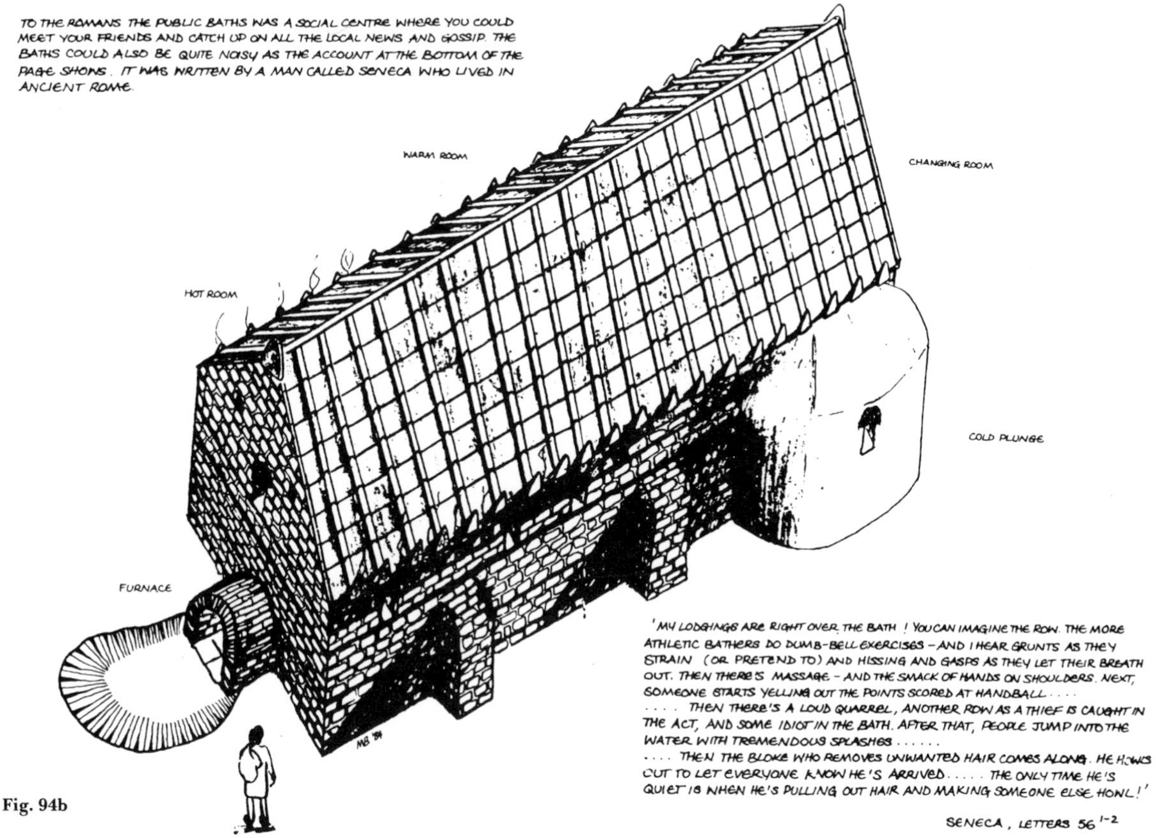

TO THE ROMANS THE PUBLIC BATHS WAS A SOCIAL CENTRE WHERE YOU COULD
MEET YOUR FRIENDS AND CATCH UP ON ALL THE LOCAL NEWS AND GOSSIP. THE
BATHS COULD ALSO BE QUITE NOISY AS THE ACCOUNT AT THE BOTTOM OF THE
PAGE SHOWS. IT WAS WRITTEN BY A MAN CALLED SENECA WHO LIVED IN
ANCIENT ROME.

WARM ROOM

CHANGING ROOM

HOT ROOM

COLD PLUNGE

FURNACE

MB '84

Fig. 94b

'MY LODGINGS ARE RIGHT OVER THE BATH! YOU CAN IMAGINE THE ROW. THE MORE
ATHLETIC BATHERS DO DUMB-BELL EXERCISES – AND I HEAR GRUNTS AS THEY
STRAIN (OR PRETEND TO) AND HISSING AND GASPS AS THEY LET THEIR BREATH
OUT. THEN THERE'S MASSAGE – AND THE SMACK OF HANDS ON SHOULDERS. NEXT,
SOMEONE STARTS YELLING OUT THE POINTS SCORED AT HANDBALL....
.... THEN THERE'S A LOUD QUARREL, ANOTHER ROW AS A THIEF IS CAUGHT IN
THE ACT, AND SOME IDIOT IN THE BATH. AFTER THAT, PEOPLE JUMP INTO THE
WATER WITH TREMENDOUS SPLASHES......
.... THEN THE BLOKE WHO REMOVES UNWANTED HAIR COMES ALONG. HE HOWLS
OUT TO LET EVERYONE KNOW HE'S ARRIVED..... THE ONLY TIME HE'S
QUIET IS WHEN HE'S PULLING OUT HAIR AND MAKING SOMEONE ELSE HOWL!'

SENECA, LETTERS 56 [1-2]

Figs. 94a and **b** The Clwyd-Powys Trust has been carrying out excavations in the seaside town of Prestatyn, in North Wales, on a Roman site which included a bath-house built close to a fort manned by soldiers of the twentieth *Legion Valeria Victrix*. Because Prestatyn is a holiday resort visited by thousands of people each year, the Trust built viewing platforms so that visitors could watch the excavation in progress, and gave guided tours. They also produced a leaflet for children, from which the drawings and text are taken. There is no doubt that most people get far more from an excavation if they have the wall foundations, post-holes and timber slots translated into three-dimensional buildings, since these are more evocative than plans or elevations, however well presented the latter are. The plan of the Prestatyn baths together with the exploded reconstruction, **Fig. 94a**, and the three-dimensional drawing of the outside, **Fig. 94b**, take the visitor step by step from the evidence on the site to the drawn and interpreted plan to the reality of the building as it was. A model or, best of all, a working full-scale replica (which might make some money for rescue archaeology!) would be even better, but these are, of course, very much more expensive and require space, permanent manning and so on. The addition in the Prestatyn guide of the list of Seneca's complaints about the baths over which he was lodging brings the bath-house vividly to life – making the local Municipal Baths seem quite sedate.
(With acknowledgements to Marion and Kevin Blockley)

also most Local Authorities subsidize or support rescue excavation to the tune of millions of pounds. To this must be added funds or help in kind given by developers in advance of the destruction which they cause. Excavators have a duty, therefore, to show the public how this money is being spent, to show that we, taxpayers all, are getting value for money in terms of new and reliable information about our past. This information must be presented in as lively and accessible a way as possible. It is not easy to conjure buildings from holes in the ground, or from pebble surfaces with straight edges, or the robber trenches of a long vanished building – to do so requires all the imagination and technical expertise in presentation that can be mustered. The methods which can be used effectively range from architectural reconstruction drawings through imaginative representation of inhabited buildings, towns and cities, scale models and full-size furnished interiors to the detailed recreation, at the Yorvik Viking Centre in York, of an inhabited village, based strictly on the excavated evidence, plus the likely sounds and smells. The discreet labels and shaven grass of English Heritage monuments will never be the same again.

The lively and imaginative presentation of excavations and excavated sites will help to convince the public and industry that archaeology is not just the private pursuit of intellectuals, but describes the past for all of us. In spite of the increase of public money spent on excavation, archaeologists have conspicuously failed to capture the imagination and the sympathy of the mass of people in the way that, for example, the bird and animal conservation societies have. Sites of the greatest interest and importance – in some cases whole landscapes – are being destroyed daily almost unnoticed; only public outcry will strengthen the law and cause it to be vigorously enforced. At the moment it is too often flouted or evaded; and the majority of all archaeological sites are not protected in any way by law. Their only hope of survival into the twenty-first century and beyond is either by a ten-fold increase in statutory protection or a vastly enhanced understanding by all concerned of the destruction that is caused by ploughing, afforestation, quarrying and rural and urban development. At the root of all this is, of course, money – the money to be made by levelling the earthworks of a deserted village, or quarrying away a hillfort, or redeveloping a historic town centre. Archaeologists can so easily be cast in the role of backward-looking fuddy-duddies, opposed to progress, wishing to fossilize the countryside and turn it into a museum. *That* we are not. But perhaps, in spite of our preoccupation with the past, we see further ahead than most, to a time when our historic roots will no longer be visible on the ground, or even under it.

EXCAVATION IN THE FUTURE

All excavation, as we have said, is destruction, and the number of archaeological sites, not only in Britain, but in the world, is diminishing daily, for a great variety of reasons. It is increasingly necessary, then, to conserve this rapidly diminishing resource and it is likely that the number of excavations, other than those carried out in advance of destruction, will decrease. As a corollary, those that are undertaken will have to be more sensitive and more efficient, extracting more reliable evidence than the best of our present excavations and subjecting that evidence to more rigorous analysis. How will this be done?

The first necessity is a rapid development of all kinds of non-destructive methods of site examination: magnetic, radar, sonar, infra-red, ultra-violet – methods, some now in their infancy, some not even yet imagined, which will enable site potential to be assessed in more reliable ways than at present. This will enable unthreatened sites to be chosen for excavation on sounder bases than at present and better choices to be made between the threatened sites.

Excavation, when it takes place, will be made much more subtle by methods of enhancement of otherwise invisible soil differences, by chemical means, by the use of lighting of different wavelengths, and, again, by means not yet thought of. The analysis of the results will, no doubt, depend more and more on computer programs of increasing subtlety and power, and on electronic methods of which holography is only the first.

Though I suspect that our chief tool, the trowel, will not be superseded for a long time, I guess that those of us digging now will be looked on as the primitives of excavation, the proto-diggers, earnest, but lacking refinement. Nevertheless, I cannot improve on Martin Carver's prediction, given to a conference on *Excavation in the 21st Century*, that ' . . . archaeological excavation will remain what it is now, the most creative, challenging and exhilarating activity that the practitioners of any discipline are priviliged to enjoy'.

If this book enables more people to understand what he means, and, even better, to join us, it will have succeeded.

GLOSSARY

aceramic   without pottery; used of periods, both historic and prehistoric, in which pottery is not used, usually in contrast with other preceding or succeeding periods, or neighbouring contemporary cultures, in which pottery is used.

anaerobic   without air; used to describe conditions, such as waterlogging, where there is insufficient oxygen for bacterial or fungal growth, so that organic materials reach a state of equilibrium beyond which they do not decay.

bailey   *see* **motte**

balk (baulk)   a strip of an archaeological site left undug to form a barrow-run, or to provide vertical **sections** (qv).

barrow-run   path created with the use of planks or tracking for the removal of spoil from the site, and for access, so that vulnerable surfaces are not damaged.

carbon-14 dating   a method of dating organic materials, such as wood, charcoal or bone, which depends on the assumption that, upon the death of a living organism, whether animal or vegetable, carbon-14 atoms present in the organism decay at a measurable rate. This dating method has undergone important modifications based on *dendrochronolgy*, or tree-ring dating. For further detail see Brothwell and Higgs, 1969, 76 ff.

crannog   an artificial platform, usually of brushwood or other timber, built in shallow water to form an island on which houses can be built.

crop-mark   crops, particularly cereals, growing over filled-in ditches, pits and gullies, tend to be more advanced, darker in colour and to ripen more quickly. This is because of the greater amounts of moisture and nutrients in these fillings. Conversely, crops growing over buried walls, floors, streets and roads will tend to be deprived of nutrients and moisture, particularly in dry weather. As a result, the crops will be thinner, and lighter in colour. The patterns thus formed can be seen from the ground, but are much better understood from the air. Examples in this book are in Figs. 19, 21-25, 26a, 30a, 30b, etc. See also D.R. Wilson *Air Photo Interpretation for Archaeologists*, Batsford, 1982.

froth flotation by adding a detergent to the water in which the soil samples are agitated, lightweight materials such as seeds and charcoal fragments can be more easily separated from the **matrix** (qv).

hachure a tapering line (tadpole) used to indicate the direction of a slope on the survey of an earthwork. The hachure points downhill and its length is related to the steepness of the slope. See Taylor, 1974 for excellent examples of hachured surveys.

iron-pan formed by iron-rich chemicals leaching through the soil and being redeposited at a lower level. Although it is a natural phenomenon, it can be mistakenly interpreted as a man-made layer, even as a floor.

levelling in the context of this book, levelling means to establish the height above site datum of a number of points (spot heights) which will either record the level of the surface of a feature or layer, or enable a contour survey to be constructed.

magnetometer an instrument for the measurement of changes in the magnetism of the earth's surface. By picking up anomalies in the earth's magnetism it can detect the presence of kilns, hearths, pits, etc.

matrix (1) the mass of material such as mud, enclosing waterlogged vegetable remains; clay containing flints, etc.
(2) by extension, the word is used to describe a pro forma of rectangles used to construct a table of the relationship of features one to another.

micro-climate the specifically local climate brought about by hills, slopes, woodland, lakes or other features of the landscape which modify the general climate of the region.

mortice a hole, usually rectangular, cut into a beam or plank, to take a *tenon*, which is a projection cut on the end of another beam and inserted into the mortice so that they can be joined together.

motte a motte is a castle mound, usually of earth, but sometimes of stone. Attached to it may be one or more baileys, which are enclosures surrounded by ramparts or stone walls.

photogrammetry the use of an overlapping stereoscopic mosaic of photographs to produce (usually with the aid of a mechanical plotter) a contour survey or elevations of a building, etc.

planum a method of digging in which horizontal slices are removed either from the whole site, or from specific features, in order to reveal a succession of plans.

pollen spectrum the diagram resulting from the analysis of the pollen from a column of peat or other soil.

post-hole; post-pipe in this book the term post-hole is used to mean the void or soil-filled mould where a post has stood. Some archaeologists use the term post-pipe to mean the same thing.

post-pit is used here to mean the pit dug to take a post. The pit is usually, though not always, bigger than its associated post-hole.

protohistoric the earliest historic periods, that is, those early periods which have documentary evidence, often minimal, relating to them.

resistivity meter a machine which measures the electrical resistivity of the earth between two probes. Since the resistivity of the soil changes with humidity, humus content, etc., the machine can detect pits, ditches, roads, floors, etc.

ring-work a defensive enclosure of bank and ditch shaped like a flan-case without the filling. This is the simplest form of defensive earthwork and can date from prehistoric times through to the Middle Ages.

robber trench the trench left (usually back-filled) by the labourers who have 'robbed' out a wall either completely or of its facing stone.

section as here used, means the stratification revealed by the cutting of a trench or other vertical face through an archaeological site.

sleeper-beam; sill-beam; cill-beam; ground-sill a horizontal foundation beam of wood, lying either directly on the ground or in a **timber-slot** (qv).

stratification the successive layers, either natural or man-made, which make up the surface of the earth, and which, in this context, are revealed by an excavation.

stratigraphy the scientific description of stratification.

thermo-luminescence a method of dating pottery and other fired materials, in which the pottery is heated until visible measurable light is emitted by released electrons; broadly speaking, the greater the age of the pot, the greater the thermo-luminescence. See Brothwell and Higgs, 1969, 106 ff.

timber-slot a trench dug to contain a horizontal beam (*see* **sleeper-beam**).

BIBLIOGRAPHY

A fuller treatment of the subject of archaeological excavation will be found in the author's *Techniques of Archaeological Excavation*, Batsford, 2nd edition, 1982, with an extensive bibliography.

In addition to those mentioned in the text, the books listed below form a short list of further reading; most of the books can be obtained through public libraries. Also recommended are the journal *Antiquity*, and the magazines, *Current Archaeology* and *Popular Archaeology*.

Recommended excavation reports are marked with *.

*Alcock, L. (1972), *By South Cadbury is that Camelot*, London

Alexander, J. (1970), *The Directing of Archaeological Excavations*, London

Aston, M. and Rowley, R.T. (1974), *Landscape Archaeology*, London

Atkinson, R.J.C. (1953), *Field Archaeology*, 2nd edition, London

*Barker, P. ed (1980) *Wroxeter Roman City, Excavations, 1966-1980*, D.O.E.

Barker, P. and Higham, R. (1982), *Hen Domen, Montgomery, A Timber Castle on the English-Welsh Border*, Vol.I. R.A.I. London

Benson, D. and Miles, D. (1974) *The Upper Thames Valley: an archaeological survey of the river gravels*, Oxford

*Beresford, G. (1975), *The Medieval Clay-Land Village: Excavations at Goltho and Barton Blount*, Society for Medieval Archaeology Monograph Series: No. 6

Beresford, M. and Hurst, J.G. (1971), *Derserted Medieval Villages*

Biddle, M. (Winchester Interim Reports) *Antiquaries Journal*, XLV (1965); XLVI (1966); XLVII (1967); XLVIII (1968); XLIX (1969); etc.

Biek, L. (1963), *Archaeology and the Microscope*, London

Binford, L.R. (1972), *An Archaeological Perspective*, New York and London

Bonnischen, Robson (1972), 'Millie's Camp: An experiment in archaeology', *World Archaeology*, 4, 277-91

Brothwell D. (1963), *Digging up Bones*, London

Brothwell, D. and Higgs, E. eds. (1969), *Science in Archaeology*, London

*Bruce-Mitford, R.L.S. ed. (1975), *Recent Archaeological Excavations in Europe*, London

Bruce-Mitford, R.L.S. (1975), *The Sutton Hoo Ship Burial*, Vol. I London

Carver, M.O.H. *Bulletin of the Sutton Hoo Research Committee*, No. 2 (1984)

Cherry, J.F., Gamble, C., and Shennan, S. (1978), *Sampling in Contemporary British Archaeology*, Oxford

Clarke, D.L. (1968), *Analytical Archaeology*, London

Coles, J. (1972), *Field Archaeology in Britain*, London

Coles, J. (1979), *Experimental Archaeology*, London

Cornwall, I. (1956), *Bones for the Archaeologist*, London

Cornwall I. (1958), *Soils for the Archaeologist*, London

Crawford, O.G.S. (1953), *Archaeology in the Field*, London

*Cunliffe, B.W. (1971), *Fishbourne, a Roman Palace and its Garden*, London

*Cunliffe, B.W. (1983), *Danebury, Anatomy of an Iron Age Hillfort*, London

Daniel, G. (1976), *A Hundred Years of Archaeology*, London

Dimbleby, G. (1967), *Plants and Archaeology*, London

Fasham, P.J., Schadla-Hall, R.T., Shennan, S.J., and Bates, P.J. (1980), *Field Walking for Archaeologists*, Andover, Hampshire

Fowler, E. ed. (1972), *Field Survey in British Archaeology*, London

Fowler, P.J. ed. (1972), *Archaeology and the Landscape*, London

Fowler, P.J. (1977), *Approaches to Archaeology*, London

Fox, Sir Cyril (1955), *Offa's Dyke*, Oxford

Greene, K. (1983), *Archaeology, An Introduction*, London

Gurney, D.A. (1985), *Phosphate Analysis of Soils: a guide for the Field Archaeologist*, Institute of Field Archaeologists Technical Paper No. 3

Harris, E.C. (1979), *Principles of Archaeological Stratigraphy*, London

Hirst, S. (1976), *Recording on Excavations I, the Written Record*, RESCUE publication No. 7, Hertford

*Hope-Taylor, B. (1977), *Yeavering, An Anglo-British centre of early Northumbria*, London, H.M.S.O.

Kenyon, Dame Kathleen (1940), 'Excavations at Viroconium, 1936-37', *Archaeologia*, 88, 175-228

Leigh, D. and others (1972), *First Aid for Finds*, Worcester

Limbrey, S. (1975), *Soil Science and Archaeology*, London

Mason and Barker (1961), 'The Norman Castle at Quatford', *Shropshire Archaeological Society Transactions*, LVIII, Part I, 37-62

Olsen, Olaf (1980) '*Rabies Archaeologorum*', *Antiquity*, 44, 15-20

Piggott, S. (1959), *Approach to Archaeology*, London

*Pitt-Rivers, A.H.L.F. (1887-98) *Excavations in Cranborne Chase*, 4 volumes, London

Rahtz, P.A. ed (1974), *Rescue Archaeology*, Harmondsworth

*Rahtz, P.A. (1979), *The Saxon and Medieval Palaces at Cheddar*, B.A.R. British Series, 65, Oxford

Rodwell, Warwick (1981), *The Archaeology of the English Church*, London

Sherratt, A. ed. (1980), *The Cambridge Encyclopedia of Archaeology*, Cambridge

Taylor, C.C. (1974), *Fieldwork in Medieval Archaeology*, London

Taylor, C.C. (1975), *Fields in the English Landscape*, London

Taylor, C.C. (1983), *Village and Farmstead*, London

van Es, W.A. (1967), 'Wijster: a Native Village beyond the Imperial Frontier 150-425 AD', *Palaeohistoria*, XI

Wheeler, R.E.M. (Sir) (1943), 'Maiden Castle, Dorset', *Society of Antiquaries*, London

Wheeler, R.E.M. (Sir) (1954), *Archaeology from the Earth*, Oxford Reprints in Pelican Books, 1956 and 1961

Wilson, D.R. (1982), *Air Photo Interpretation for Archaeologists*, London

Wright, Thomas (1872), *Uriconium*

INDEX